CHAKRAKEY™
A KEY FOR HUMANITY

Rick Ireton

The image shown on the cover, *ChakraSynergy*, is a reproduction of a crop circle found in a field of barley, May 25, 2009 at Windmill Hill, near Devizes Wilts, UK. The symbol has been colorized and placed over a man sitting in the lotus position. This amazing image illustrates the movement of bio-energy as it flows throughout the human body, and reveals to us the nature of our human spiritual design.

The following terms are proprietary marks of the author:

ChakraSynergy **is a registered trademark of Love, Peace and Freedom Foundation.**

ChakraKey **is a trademark of Love, Peace and Freedom Foundation.**

To enhance readability, the symbols ® and TM have been omitted from the body of this work.

ISBN: 978-0-9891894-0-8

Published by the Love, Peace and Freedom Foundation.

LOVE, PEACE & FREEDOM
FOUNDATION

http://www.lovepeaceandfreedom.org/
2033 San Elijo Ave. # 122
Cardiff, CA 92007

As ever so slowly it might seem, we are evolving into love.
The gravitational force of the heart is pulling us surely and steadily
into the ocean of love. New images emerge to help
us see through the fog of confusion, and onto a path of new thought,
illuminated by the light of love.

– Rick Ireton

I thought I knew

Now I know

The Rainbow, Mother Nature's Symbol of Love!

DEDICATION

This book is dedicated to my brothers and sisters of the light.
It is through the power of your love that we will transform
our world into heaven here on Earth.

ACKNOWLEDGMENTS

The ChakraKey was created from years of research on the topics of love and chakras. This book is not intended to be a comprehensive exposition about chakras, but a "User Guide" for the human spiritual being.

I offer many thanks to my friend Jim Byer, for setting me on the path to love, and for sharing his great wisdom about the natural sciences and our bodies' natural drives. Thanks also to my friends Vlad Ghiulamila, Nayan Bliss, Sandra Hartwell, and Susan Robertson, for your most valuable help exploring with me the deeper meaning of life and love, and to Sheila Moore of Aura Explorations and Savitri Simpson, for information about chakras and the human aura.

It should be noted, the study of chakras is a science of the mystics, and there is a variety of opinion as to the function and purpose of our inner design. The ChakraKey and ChakraSynergy symbols bring us more pieces of the puzzle, advancing our understanding our Divine nature.

CONTENTS

Author's Preface

How I Found Love

As sales manager of a small graphic design company, I enjoy the good fortune of having my office located near the beach in Southern California. Back in 2002, I spent many a lunch hour walking on the beach with my friend Jim. We would discuss politics, religion, and current events of the day. Jim is a renaissance man, who in many ways is the smartest person I have ever met. As we set off for our walk one particular afternoon, I had a burden to share. I had recently observed abortion protestors at a nearby location, holding large signs with pictures of aborted fetuses. The images were graphic and horrendous. I was deeply affected by these scenes. Discouraged by the complexity of the abortion issue, I was looking forward to talking with Jim about this most complex and perplexing matter.

As we set off for our walk that afternoon, I said, "Jim, there just doesn't seem to be any answer to the abortion issue. Both sides make valid points. Both sides seem right, yet they cannot both be right. There must be some reasonable answer to this complicated issue."

Without giving the matter much thought, Jim said, "It's easy, you make LOVE first." F.I.R.S.T. is an acronym Jim came up with that stands for Fair, Integral, Related, Systems of Thought. I did not grasp the meaning of his acronym for a while. Jim explained further. "Love weighs all things. The only fair way to address the abortion issue is to look at each and every pregnancy on an individual basis. There are just too many circumstances surrounding each pregnancy to make a hard and fast rule that would apply to every circumstance."

This reasoning certainly made sense to me. How could we make a single rule that would apply to every pregnancy? In the world of right and wrong, it would be convenient to have a black and white rule stating, 'this is right and that is wrong.' Unfortunately, we live in a complex world, with complex issues that require a greater wisdom and responsibility from each person. There are many important dilemmas we face in life that require a depth of understanding and wisdom. It is only through the eyes of love, that can we access the great depth, width, and breadth of Divine wisdom we need to help us make the most important decisions of our lives.

I learned something that day that had never before occurred to me. *Love* is the answer, and *love weighs all things*. This new revelation was an "aha" moment for me. If love was the answer to the abortion issue, imagine all of the other issues that love might resolve. So what is love? I could not define love in that moment. I knew however that love is a subject worth further investigation. Could the answer to the many issues we face in life be as simple as love? The idea seemed plausible. With a newly piqued curiosity, I made a decision to look into this matter of *love*.

Putting the Pieces Together

For the next ten years, I sought out and read everything I could find about love. Through books, conversations, experiences, and writing, I began to envision a book about love. Knowing the value of good visual imagery, my first thought was to make a picture book illustrating the virtues of love. What could be more telling of love than a photo of a mother holding her young child? The more I learned of love, the more books emerged from my imagination. The *Virtues of Love* book evolved into *Conditions of the Heart*, and that turned into *The Love Manifesto*, then *Earth School*, and finally *ChakraKey*. With each new revelation of love came a fresh perspective and application for love's wisdom.

I made the connection between the chakra system and the menorah in 2010 after I was about eight years into my study. I learned of the seven-candle menorah from my friend Jim who would often speak of the Jewish menorah and the significance of number seven. I discovered the relationship between the menorah and the chakra system by simply turning an image of the menorah sideways, and placing it next to an image of the human chakra system. While looking at the two images, I noticed how the center mast of the menorah aligned with the heart chakra, and its branches aligned with the upper and lower chakras. Upon closer inspection of the branches, a map emerged of the interconnecting points between the upper and lower chakra system. I knew then that these two symbols were meant to be together. You can see the interlinking pattern of colors in the ChakraKey on the back cover of the book.

ChakraKey marries Hindu wisdom of the chakra system with the seven-candle menorah from the Jewish tradition. Hindu wisdom lays the foundation of thought about chakras, and the menorah provides a map illustrating the interconnections between the heart chakra, and upper and lower chakras. When we combine Hindu wisdom of the chakra system with the ChakraKey, we are provided with new wisdom about our human spiritual design, our purpose in life, and our interconnection with Mother Nature's rainbow.

Once I found the connection between the menorah and the chakra system, other pieces of the puzzle began to emerge. While researching chakras, I discovered the "ChakraSynergy" crop circle. As I was flipping through images of crop circles, one image caught my attention. When

I counted the seven energetic centers of the symbol, I realized this was another visual representation of the chakra system. While examining this new symbol, I was struck by the large heart chakra center. "Wow," I thought. "Look at the size of our heart chakra. This symbol illustrates the power of love within each of us." After further investigation of the symbol, I came up with the name ChakraSynergy. The name seemed fitting because the symbol gives us an illustration of the word synergy. Synergy is defined as *The working together of two or more energies when the result is greater than the sum of their individual effects or capabilities.*

The ChakraKey and ChakraSynergy symbols provide us with two unique views of our unseen energy body and untold information about our human spiritual design. The ChakraKey illustrates the interconnections of the upper and lower chakras, and the ChakraSynergy symbol gives us a diagram illustrating the directional movement of bioenergy as it moves throughout the human body.

Another amazing discovery I made during my study was the connection between the pattern of colors within the chakra system, the rainbow, and the prism. Mother Nature's organizational framework of design can be clearly seen within the pattern of colors found in the rainbow, the chakra system, and the prism. The menorah provides us with a key to understand the interrelationships between these energy patterns.

Yet another important piece of the puzzle is found in our connection to the music scale. Based on a hunch, I thought perhaps there was a relationship between the pattern of colors in the rainbow and music. My research turned up Isaac Newton's theory of music. Newton discovered the relationship between the color spectrum and music hundreds of years ago.

Newton divided the spectrum into seven named colors: red, orange, yellow, green, blue, indigo, and violet. He chose seven colors out of a belief, derived from the ancient Greek sophists, that there was a connection between the colors, the musical notes, the known objects in the solar system, and the days of the week.

Seven is indeed a magic number for us. Seven is the number of nature's natural harmony.

Seven Chakras

Seven major colors in the Rainbow and Prism

Seven notes in the major musical scale

Seven days of the week

Seven branches of the Menorah

As we assemble pieces of the human puzzle, a new picture begins to emerge of the human spiritual being, and of our purpose in life.

- Hindu wisdom lays the foundation of thought about chakras.
- ChakraKey shows us how spirit and flesh are joined together as one.
- ChakraSynergy illustrates the movement of our bio-energetic design.
- The pattern of colors in the rainbow and prism illustrates our connection to Mother Nature.
- The notes within our music scale enable us to hear the sound of harmony we can see in the rainbow.
- Love is at the heart of the matter.

The reality of our spiritual nature and connection to Mother Nature should not be a mystery. We intuitively know that we are more than flesh and bones, yet up until now, we have lacked evidence and understanding of this connection. We now have a diagram, as clear as the colors within the rainbow. This is exciting news for all of us. We no longer need to grope around in the dark, looking for the meaning of life. Two new symbols provide us with logical answers to the questions we have been looking for. We now have tangible evidence proving our divine nature.

ChakraKey is a spiritual adventure, an awakening for all. Beginning as children, we grow and evolve as we process new information and understanding of our world. Wisdom provided by the ChakraKey is new information that will change your perspective about the nature of humanity, the meaning of life, and the great potential that lies within each of us. Knowledge is power. With spiritual awareness comes new spiritual power and abilities. Understanding this information is vital for humanity to evolve in a loving way. Without knowledge and understanding of the basic truths of life, we are easily manipulated by primal thinking people, who seek to replace love with fear and doubt, taking any advantage for their own personal gain.

Knowledge is the key to love, peace, and prosperity.

I am anxious for you to read this information, knowing that it will set your life on a new course of evolution. The most amazing adventure one might ever experience is exploring one's own heart and inner being. As you come into alignment with your greater integrity, you will find your life fills with greater love, meaning and purpose.

We are here for love.
May we together gather around her and never let go.

Rick Ireton, Cardiff, California

INTRODUCTION

As a garden has many unique flowers, we are many unique souls,
here on Earth to bud and blossom in our own unique way.

You hold in your hand a key to the most valuable treasure you might ever gain: *Love, Knowledge, Wisdom, and Truth.* What is more important than love, truth, and the body of inner wisdom you hold within your consciousness? What thing in life will serve you more than understanding the world in light of truth, knowledge, and wisdom? Truth being that which is everlasting, constant, and permanent. What could be more important than an understanding of the meaning of life, based upon scientific evidence that we can see the rainbow, and observe with objective reasoning?

ChakraKey reveals the human-spiritual design. Through the marriage of two ancient symbols, and one symbol recently found in the form of a crop circle, ChakraKey makes known that which was unknowable. Symbols are powerful teaching tools that speak in every language through their unique design. ChakraKey is an educational tool that reveals the energetic nature of our human-spiritual design, and thus our purpose in life. It is through understanding and awareness of our human spiritual nature that we are able to manage our bodies and live in the light of love as spiritual beings. We are indeed a great society of loving spiritual beings, here for a greater purpose of love.

ChakraKey is the Rosetta Stone of spirituality. Egyptian hieroglyphics were a mystery until the discovery of the Rosetta Stone, upon which King Ptolemy V's decree appears in three languages; Ancient Greek, Demotic, and Ancient Egyptian hieroglyphs. Because scholars understood Ancient Greek, they had a reference to translate the unknown. As the Rosetta Stone is the key to translating a mysterious past, ChakraKey allows us to see that which is invisible, and to decode the inner programming of our human spiritual bodies. The seekers who came upon the Rosetta Stone unlocked a door of history. ChakraKey unlocks a door to the future.

If humanity is to evolve in a loving way, it will happen because we discover the truth of our human spiritual nature. As a human family, we share the same framework of design, and we all have what is called a bio-energetic or chakra system. *While we each have a body, we are not the body.* We are spiritual beings of Divine creation, each with a body vehicle for the purpose of our greater expression. Our objective in life is to be an expression of our spiritual nature while understanding and managing our physical bodies. Without the knowledge of our human spiritual design, we are lost in a world of confusion. How long has humankind sought to understand the true meaning of life? For a thousand generations we have toiled under the feet of oppressive leaders, governments, and religions. How many fine, loving people have come into this world with hopes and dreams of living out happy, joy-filled lives; only to be killed in war, die of starvation or endure a life filled with pain and frustration?

The ChakraKey and the ChakraSynergy symbols together provide us with a wealth of information far beyond my understanding. I am honored to present my thoughts on the ChakraKey, and how we might share a greater love for one another. The pursuit of love is the key for us here. Love has been off our radar for so long, yet it is the single most important topic we might consider.

While chakras are not visible for most people (there are some seers and mystics able to perceive them), they are energy centers within the human body. We all have them. Understanding these centers and their function is fundamental to inner personal growth. Why is this information important? Understanding our inner design is as important as understanding how to operate a computer. Many people use computers without the slightest knowledge of how they actually work. We do the same thing in life, with ourselves! We are very concerned with our outward look and performance but have little or no knowledge of the inner workings – of the software, so to speak. Before we can take full advantage of our spiritual hardware, we must understand our inner programming and system features. Hindu wisdom of chakras, and the symbols within the ChakraKey provides us with important information about our inner design that we need to know. The wants of the body are powerful, and they are not always in our best interest! The better we understand our spiritual /physical equipment, the better we will do in life. Knowledge is the key to inner personal growth, peace, and harmony. Through the knowledge, wisdom, and understanding of ChakraKey, we can evolve our lives from a survival-based flailing, into spiritual lives filled with love, meaning, and purpose.

ChakraKey provides us with evidence of our Divine nature that we can actually experience. Spiritual awareness is not an ethereal concept, but a reality we can consciously experience at any given moment. As multi-dimensional human beings, we are able to objectively experience our spiritual selves.

Sometimes, the most important discoveries we make in life are the simple things right in front of us. It is comforting to know that life does make sense. The pattern of colors we see in the rainbow is the same pattern of colors within our chakra system, the prism, the atom, and the grandest galaxy in the universe. We are not here as random accidents. We are all here for a reason. It is time that we understand what that reason is, so we might begin living and not just existing.

If we are in fact spiritual beings, then the possibilities of our past, present, and future are quite remarkable. Who knows where we may have been, what we may have been through, and where we are heading?

One day, we will each say goodbye to our bodies, but we will not be dead. We will be moving on to another classroom. Our souls learn through experience. The way we spend our limited time here on Earth matters. It is in our best interest to look at life as a great classroom, and spend our time well. We have many lessons to learn, and in this present reality it appears that the course is called, "The Theory and Practice of Love." You hold in your hands a guidebook to use for your own personal discovery.

The ChakraKey presents a new, love-based philosophy for life, based upon our human spiritual design, our connection to Mother Nature's rainbow, and love. As human spiritual beings, we are designed for a purpose. Our purpose in life should naturally follow our form, as represented by each of our chakras.

The ChakraKey is a book for spiritual students and teachers who seek a greater understanding of the meaning of life. If we are to evolve in a loving way here on Earth, we will do so because we grow in knowledge of our spiritual nature, and begin to love and honor one another as the kind and gentle people we truly are.

This book includes a Personal Assessment that will help you become a greater expression of your higher nature. The assessment is a series of questions for you to reflect upon, to help you discover your physical and spiritual gifts. We are all incredibly gifted people. Often, our physical and spiritual abilities are so great; that it is difficult to choose which ones we will share with others. As we assess our many gifts, may we give greater consideration to the higher aspirations of our spirit nature.

As there are many unique and beautiful flowers in God's nature, we are many unique and beautiful souls, here on Earth to bring some experience to light, to learn, to grow, and to help others grow in their own unique ways.

PART ONE

THE MEANING OF LIFE

"You are not a human being in search of a spiritual experience.
You are a spiritual being immersed in a human experience."

– Teilhard de Chardin

There is a wonderful story that has been told for generations about a man who stepped out for an evening walk, only to come across a man searching for his keys under the streetlights. He offers to help him search, and so they get down on their hands and knees. After a long while, the passer-by asks the man, "Are you sure you lost them here?" to which the other man replies, "No, but there is more light out here under the streetlights."

It is common to only give our attention to areas of our lives with which we are familiar, rather than to grope around areas that are foreign and uncertain, even if they hold the answer. What prevents us from moving forward, is our lack of understanding our true identity, and fear of what we might become if we allow ourselves to embrace the unknown.

So where do we begin? Knowledge is the key. Every great leap in human development has come about through a new understanding. This book deals with the fundamental questions we must resolve, in order to set a new intention for the evolution of humankind. No matter who you are, which country you live in, or what beliefs you hold about life, the one mystery that all humanity and all generations share, is one of *identity and purpose.*

ChakraKey provides us with a wondrous yet logical explanation of who we are, and why we are here. Our purpose in life is clearly found in our human spiritual design.

Who am I?

Who are you?

What is the meaning of life?

I am ... you are ... we are all spiritual beings having a human experience.

As spirit beings, we all have a body.

We are two dynamic creations within one body; one is seen, the other is unseen.

The human body provides spirit with a vehicle for its expression, and a medium through which to shine. We are spiritual matter, drops of Divine energy seeking to shine the light that is within us through our physical/spiritual existence.

Our exquisite bodies are animated by the unseen electromagnetic energy of our spirit selves. We are so completely perfectly made; that we are often unaware of our Divine nature.

What is the meaning of life? As spiritual beings, we are here as students and teachers for the purpose of inner personal growth, spiritual evolution, and to be expressions of our Divine nature. As a diamond has many unique facets of light, we are many unique facets of spirit, manifesting light in our own unique ways.

Knowledge is power. We are empowered by spiritual awareness. Once we discover the truth of our spiritual identity, we can understand why we behave, feel, and act the way we do. It is only after we understand the nature of our physical / spiritual relationship that we can take control of our bodies, our emotions, and thus our lives. It is through spiritual awakening that we can establish new motives and objectives for our lives. This recognition begins the real point of change for each of us. Once we know, we begin to grow.

Black, white, red, or brown, we are all made with the same building materials; we feel the same pains and strive for the same love. It is time for us all to realize the unity we share, that we might increase our radiance through an ever-expansive love for one another. Our common goal is to raise consciousness within the human family. We are all here for family: to love, to be loved, to learn, to teach, and to grow.

As spiritual students and teachers, we each come into this world with a unique lesson plan for our life. As we grow in life, love has her way of crafting us into the unique flowers we are destined to become. We are all in transition. As students, we accelerate our lesson plans by:

- Understanding the nature of our bodies
- Understanding the nature of love
- Understanding our spiritual nature
- Choosing to love and to be loved
- Making decisions based on loving intuition
- Discovering God's love in all things, every minute, and everywhere

The goal is to expand awareness.
We do better when we know better.

THE MENORAH
THE "DIVINE PATTERN"

*"And in the midst of the seven candlesticks,
one is like unto the Son of man."*

Revelations 1:13

The *menorah* is the Hebrew term for the seven-branched lampstand.
The Bible tells us that God revealed a specific design for the menorah to
Moses and describes its construction. (Exodus 25:31-40)

*31 "Make a lampstand of pure, hammered gold. The entire lampstand and
its decorations will be one piece – the base, center stem, lamp cups, buds, and
blossoms. 32 It will have six branches; three branches going out from each
side of the center stem. 33 Each of the six branches will hold a cup shaped
like an almond blossom, complete with buds and petals. 34 The center stem of
the lampstand will be decorated with four almond blossoms, complete with
buds and petals. 35 One blossom will be set beneath each pair of branches
where they extend from the center stem. 36 The decorations and branches
must all be one piece with the stem, and they must be hammered from pure
gold. 37 Then make the seven lamps for the lampstand, and set them so
they reflect their light forward. 38 The lamp snuffers and trays must also*

*be made of pure gold. **39** You will need seventy-five pounds of pure gold for the lampstand and its accessories. **40** Be sure that you make everything according to the pattern I have shown you here on the mountain.*

The menorah described in the book of Exodus has many features not shown in the above illustration. There was more to the menorah than we may ever know. What we can see, however, that is meaningful, is the *Divine pattern* illustrated within the branches. The significance of the menorah design becomes apparent when an image of the lampstand is turned sideways and placed next to an image of the human chakra system. The center mast of the menorah clearly aligns with the heart chakra, and the branches align with the upper and lower chakras. When we apply Hindu wisdom of the chakra system with the branches of the menorah, we are provided with the energetic design of the human spiritual body. In essence, we are given a picture of how the spiritual body interlinks with the physical body. While we can see the physical body, our energetic design is beyond our ability of comprehension, yet understanding of this design is fundamental to our spiritual growth and evolution.

ARCH OF TITUS

COURTESY: BIBLE HISTORY ONLINE

The *Arch of Titus*, shown above, is home to one of the earliest stone carvings of the menorah. The relief can be seen in the upper right-hand corner of the arch.

Stone Carving Replica

Courtesy: Bible History online

The image above is a photographic replica of the relief carving found in the Arch of Titus.

The Roman soldiers above are shown carrying the seven-branched candelabrum or menorah through the streets of Rome after the Jewish defeat in A.D. 70. It is one of the earliest recorded menorah designs available today. Note the large central staff supporting the six branches.

The menorah is the key to one of the greatest mysteries of our time, and it has been hiding in plain sight for thousands of years.

CHAKRAS 101

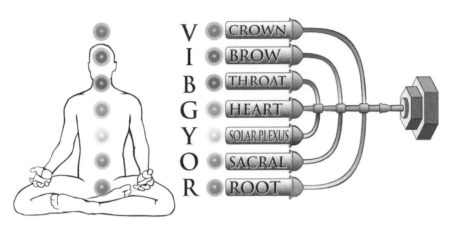

The man sitting above illustrates the general location
and color of each of chakra.
ROYGBIV is an abbreviation for each color.
Red, Orange, Yellow, Green, Blue, Indigo, Violet

What are chakras? Chakras are unseen energy centers within each human body. Each center has a unique vibration, color, sound and guiding intelligence.

Unlocking the mystery of the ChakraKey begins with understanding the basics of chakras. While modern seekers have some intuitive sense of our inner design; our knowledge is but foam on the ocean. As energetic human beings, we are very powerful; so much so, that new imaging systems are able to photograph the human aura and chakra system. (For more information about these systems see Chakra Imaging Systems.)

The word *chakra* is Sanskrit for the word "wheel," so named by Hindu mystics who were able, during mediation, to observe spinning vortices of light energy within their bodies.

- Each human has seven major chakra centers.
- Each chakra has a resonant energy. We are able to measure this energy as a color.
- Chakras are not part of the physical body. They can move around as our energy moves.
- Chakras are intersecting energy points of the subtle body the masters call, "nadis."

When a human body is healthy, energy or prana from the seven chakras runs freely throughout the body, just as water runs through an irrigation trough. If one of the channels is blocked, we can become very sick and even die. While the chakras are a mysterious aspect of our human nature, they cannot be denied. We can measure chakra energy with electronic equipment and see them with sensitive cameras; however, we cannot identify a physical part of the human body and call it a chakra.

"Prana is the basic component of your subtle body, your energy field, and entire chakra system... the key to life and source of energy in the universe."

– Shumsky

Where are the chakras? The spinal centers, or chakras, are found at the points where tributary streams of energy (prana or life force) from the body, join the awakened, upward flow of energy in the deep or astral spine. The astral, or energy, spine is not the backbone (those knobs that can be felt along the back), but runs more or less through the center of the body. Energy flows through the central nervous system and through the astral spine. In our un-awakened state, the main energy flow is downward, away from the brain, and outward to the organs and limbs.

– Savitri Simpson, Chakras for Starters

Understanding the human chakra system is fundamental to personal development. While some things in life are obvious to us, such as our five senses, some very important functions of our bodies fly below the level of our consciousness. The chakra system is one of the most important features of our bodies, yet the subject is not covered within our institutions or acknowledged by doctors.

Could you imagine trying to fix a computer control system on a new car without a blueprint or any knowledge of how it works? Our chakra system is like a computer control system in a modern car, only much more complex. As a car has many systems for the engine, brakes, and lights, a human body has seven major systems.

The ChakraKey and ChakraSynergy symbols provide us with new information about the design of our energy bodies that is beyond intuitive reasoning until you see the design and then it all makes sense.

How does the chakra system affect the body? Each chakra is associated with one of our seven glands. Glands secrete hormones into the bloodstream as directed by thought, via the chakra system. If our lives are in danger and our greater thought is to run, energy is channeled into the root chakra, energizing the adrenal glands to secrete adrenaline into our bloodstreams so that we might run to escape from harm.

Each of our chakra centers serves our bodies for a specific purpose. Each color carries a unique wave pattern and intelligence. Together they enable us to survive and to flourish as human spiritual beings. We are designed to be the accumulative expression of our chakras. As we evaluate our physical and spiritual design, it becomes clear that love is at the heart of the matter.

CHAKRA AWARENESS EXERCISE

Although chakras are invisible to our physical senses, we are able to perceive each chakra center if we take a moment to consider them. Use the exercise below to feel and experience each chakra center. Direct your attention to each chakra center to feel the energy.

Crown chakra – Close your eyes, bring your attention to the top of your head and feel the energy. Rest for a moment in prayer with gratitude for your life and say "thank you." This high center is our spiritual antenna and point of connection with the Divine.

Brow chakra – Once again close your eyes. Bring your inner gaze to the space between your eyebrows and visualize a waterfall. Can you smell the mist and hear its sound? All of the activity of seeing, hearing, smelling, thinking, imagination, and creativity happen in this center.

Throat chakra – Now bring your attention to your throat area and say something, or sing a melody for a moment. Feel the energy in your throat chakra and chest area. How vital is this center to our life experience? Our inner power is manifest through our voice.

Heart chakra – Now think of touching or holding someone you love. Can you feel this energy in your heart? The heart is our most powerful center. We know love because we can feel it. You can send anybody love energy even if you do not know them.

Solar plexus chakra – The Solar plexus is located just below your rib cage. Bring your attention to this area and imagine you have a pocket full of money. Think of the security and confidence this energy brings you. Money equals power and security and feels good.

Sacral chakra – Dropping your attention now to just below your belly button, recall the pleasure this energetic center has brought you. We are designed to seek that which feels good.

Root chakra – Now bring your attention to your lowest center, and imagine having to run for your life for some reason. Can you feel the energy of fear coming from this area?

We are mostly unaware of this most important and powerful center, yet our greatest drive is to survive.

Finding your chakras is like finding a new group of friends; one primal, one sexual, one powerful, one loving, one compassionate, one communicative, one thoughtful, and one spiritual. The ones we give our attention to, get our energy. As we grow in awareness of each center, we can choose to spend our time and energy in the centers that best serve our greater health, wealth, and joy. We can consciously choose love and higher vitality.

Where your attention goes, your energy flows.
Manage your attention, manage your energy.

WHAT ARE CHAKRA DRIVES?

CROWN- GOD
BROW-WISDOM
THROAT- COMMUNICATION
HEART- LOVE
SOLAR PLEXUS- POWER
SACRAL- SEX
ROOT- SURVIVAL

*It is only after we understand the nature
of our human spiritual design that we are able
to transform ourselves into fully integrated spiritual beings.*

What are drives? The term *drive* gives us a word picture to help us understand the driving propensity of each chakra. Each chakra is a powerful energy system for the body, and each system serves a specific purpose. Like a hard drive within a computer system, each chakra carries resonant energy and stores memory. Given our great drive for balance, each center records everything associated with each particular drive, so we might survive and thrive as a species.

It's hard to fathom the nature of our inner programming. While we are here on Earth to live, to love, to learn, to grow, and to express, we first must survive in what is sometimes a hostile environment. To do all of this, our creator has given us a control system with seven primary drive systems. Below is a list of each chakra's natural drive.

Root chakra – Drive for survival

Sacral chakra – Drive for sex and pleasure

Solar plexus – Drive for social power and to maintain resources for survival

Heart chakra – Drive for love, compassion, harmony, and balance

Throat chakra – Drive for communication, inspiration, logical understanding

Brow chakra – Drive for intuition, knowledge, wisdom, perception, and creativity

Crown chakra – Drive for spirituality, freedom, wholeness, and enlightenment

We are complex creatures, yet we manage seven powerful centers without much effort, awareness, or difficulty. However, we are only able to ascend into the higher chakras once we are safe, fed, warm, healthy, and in a loving environment. These basics are fundamental to inner personal growth.

WHAT ARE HUMAN PREFERENCES?

A preference within a computer system is a setting that allows one to establish a preferred method of operation for a particular piece of hardware or software. A human preference is something we prefer for some reason. Our preferences become our habits, and our habits define our lives.

Early in life, we begin to determine what we like and dislike. Some of our preferences are established for very good reasons, and others are based on bad information. For example, imagine for a moment that you are a young child who is given milk with sugar in the baby bottle. While the sweet milk tastes delicious, the sugar in the milk can lead to tooth decay and other health problems. Your mother unknowingly has helped you establish an unhealthy preference for sugar. Not all things that taste good are good for us, even though they may seem so on the surface.

We often determine what is good or bad for us by examining very little information. Once a preference is set, and the program is recorded within the body, setting a new preference can be a challenge. Consider for a moment all of the many preferences you have for things. As an exercise, consider the many preferences you have established within each of your chakra centers. Beginning with your root chakra, think about where your next drink of water will come from? What kind of water is it? is it filtered or from the tap? We make thousands of decisions large and small every day. From the very basic to the sublime, our preferences are part of our survival and greater intelligence.

Establishing healthful preferences is important to our well-being and survival. Our preferences become our habits, and our habits determine the outcome of our lives. Making good decisions for our lives requires that we understand a vast amount of information about all of the many things that affect us. Good information is the key to establishing healthy preferences. When we know what is good and why it is good, we can choose what is good.

Awareness changes everything. If we learn early in life that we are Divinely created spiritual beings, and we establish healthful preferences for body, mind, and spirit, we will naturally become the preferred vision of who we are as spirit beings. Once we discover our spiritual gifts and learn that it is OK and right for us to use these gifts, we can adjust our preferences to refining our higher aspirations. As we grow in knowledge and wisdom about the body, spirit relationship and the nature of our purpose in life, we can prefer to become the higher vision of our selves. It is all a matter of perspective.

PART TWO:
DECODING THE CHAKRAKEY

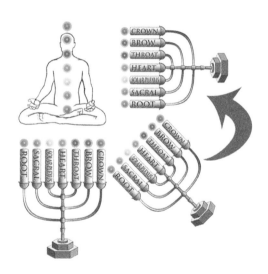

Turn the key, to solve the mystery!

The seven-candle menorah becomes a key or diagram of the human chakra system when turned sideways and placed next to an image representing Hindu wisdom of the chakra system. In this chapter, we will decode the mystery of the human Chakra system.

THE CHAKRAKEY MENORAH

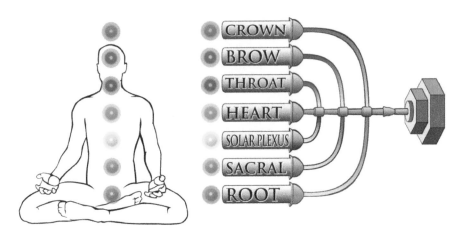

*The ChakraKey shows us how spirit and flesh
are joined together as one.*

The illustration above is of a man sitting in the lotus position with chakra centers illuminated. Next to the man is an illustration of the seven-candle menorah. When the menorah is turned sideways and placed next to the seven energetic points of the human chakra system, a map is revealed illustrating the interconnections between the heart chakra and the upper and lower chakras. For clarity, each candle is color coded and labeled with the corresponding chakra.

The ChakraKey is a teaching tool to help us understand the design of our human spiritual bodies. Our human spiritual design is revealed by applying Hindu wisdom of the chakra system, with the programming code provided by the menorah. Awareness of our inner programming is fundamental to spiritual growth.

ChakraKey Basics:

- The center mast of the menorah corresponds with the heart chakra

- The three lower branches correspond with the lower chakras
- The three upper branches correspond with the upper chakras
- The branches illustrate each chakra connection.

Root/heart/crown chakra connection – The lower branch of the menorah illustrates the connection between the root chakra and the crown chakra, via the heart chakra. Our root chakra has to do with our connection to Earth and survival. Our crown chakra is our energetic connection with the Divine.

Sacral/heart/brow chakra connection – The center branch of the menorah illustrates the connection between our sacral chakra and the brow chakra, through the heart chakra. Our lower chi forces are gathered in this low center to power our most amazing minds.

Solar plexus/heart/throat chakra connection – The inner branch of the menorah illustrates the connection between our solar plexus chakra and our throat chakra, through the heart chakra. Our solar plexus provides the forces needed for our voices, our true source of power.

Heart chakra connections – The center mast of the menorah represents the heart chakra center, from which the upper and lower chakras draw their power. Our heart chakra is the radiant source of energy for our chakra system.

Spirit and flesh are joined together as one body through the chakra system. Each chakra serves a specific purpose for our survival and life experience.

Looking at the ChakraKey, one can see the logical framework of thought that has gone into our human spiritual design. In the ranking and organization of needs, our most basic desire would be to first seek out food, water, shelter, and the things we need to survive. Once these were secured, one would seek a mate and then build walls for security. Living on Earth is wild and dangerous!

The ChakraKey gives us a diagram of two systems governed by a larger center. A trinity of lower yang energies is connected at the heart to be used by a trinity of yin energy.

- Our drive for survival is influenced by our connection to the Divine.
- Our drive for sex and pleasure is influenced by our logical thinking mind
- Our drive for personal power is influenced by our greater understanding.
- Our great heart is designed to maintain our chakra system in a state of equilibrium.

When Hindu wisdom of the chakra system is combined with the Hebrew menorah, as shown in the ChakraKey, we are provided with the hierarchy of the human spiritual design. There is intelligent reasoning to our design, of course. We are more than flesh and bones. The more we understand our energetic design, the better we will be able to understand and manage our spiritual equipment.

ROOT/HEART/CROWN CHAKRA CONNECTION

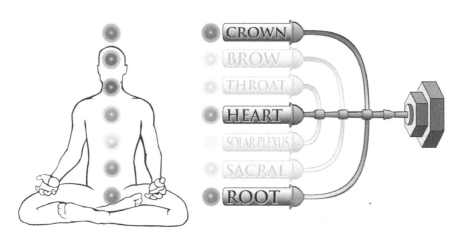

The root / heart / crown chakra connection is illustrated
by the bottom branch from the root chakra, to the heart chakra,
to the top branch at the crown chakra.

The root/heart/crown chakra connection illustrates our connection to Divine consciousness from the root of our being. From Heaven to Earth, and Earth to Heaven, we are energetically connected to Divine intelligence!

- Root chakra connects us to the Earth and drives us to seek out the things we need to survive such as air, water, food, warmth, safety, sleep, and shelter.

- The upper branch illustrates our connection with Divine consciousness. All of our thoughts, pains, joy, and actions are known by our creator. It's useless to run, and we cannot hide. We live in glass houses. There are no secrets. We are open books. Life is about learning the many lessons of life and love.

- We are each like a personal computer plugged into Divine consciousness. We are always plugged in and connected to the source.

- The root chakra is a red energy vibration that provides our bodies with energetic life force. The blood that flows in our bodies is red.

- As with one, so is all of humanity. The rules we identify as true with the body and spirit are the rules for our lives and our civilization.

SACRAL/HEART/BROW CHAKRA CONNECTION

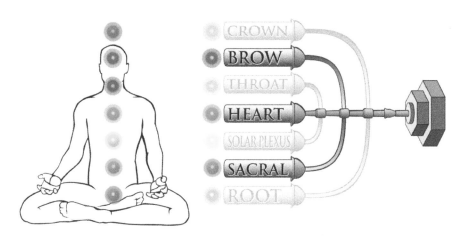

The sacral / heart / brow chakra connection is illustrated by the branch from the sacral chakra, to the heart chakra, to the branch from the brow chakra.

The sacral chakra is the axis point of our lower chakra system, and the brow chakra is the axis point of our upper chakra system. The menorah provides us with a diagram illustrating the energetic connection between these two powerful centers.

- The brow chakra/mind requires a steady, reliable source of energy. This energy source is provided by the lower chi forces, gathered in the sacral chakra. The lower chakras serve the upper chakras.

- Our powerful drive for sex is kept influenced the heart chakra and our logical thinking mind. Without knowledge and understanding of this powerful drive, our animal passions can overpower our better judgment. This is a great stumbling block for most of humanity. If we are here to honor one another in a healthful way, we must grow in awareness of this most important center.

- **Gut intuition.** As Divine wisdom channels into our crown and brow chakras, it is laid to rest in our gut. Isn't it interesting how our inner knowing comes not only from our great minds but also from within our lower center?

The spinning energy from this powerful center helps us find balance in a world of duality. With all of the many options this world has to offer, we are able to master our environment, seeking things that bring us a pleasurable experience.

SOLAR PLEXUS/HEART/THROAT CHAKRA CONNECTION

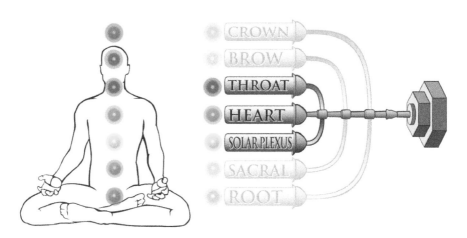

The solar plexus / heart / throat chakra connection is illustrated by the branch from the solar plexus, to the heart chakra, to the branch from the throat chakra.

To feel the physical sensation of this energetic connection, push on your solar plexus and feel air rush to your voice.

- The air we breathe that powers our body, gathers in the solar plexus. This air provides us with our great power expression through our voice and fifth chakra.

- Our great drive for personal power and security is found in the solar plexus. Once man has secured the necessities of survival, he is compelled to build walls to protect the resources he has gathered.

- Drive for social power. In our quest for survival, it is our nature to seek security and acceptance within the human group. While our drive for power and security is natural and a good thing, we must manage this drive with a greater drive for love, balance, and compassion for one another. The drive for power has been a stumbling block for humanity since the beginning of time. How much is enough? At what point are we secure?

Man's never-ending quest for power is responsible for the downfall of God's creation throughout time. We take control of this obsessive behavior by understanding the origin of this energy, accepting its manifestation, and then manage it.

Our challenge is to overcome our fear of lack of resources needed for our survival, comfort and creative expression.

HEART CHAKRA CONNECTIONS

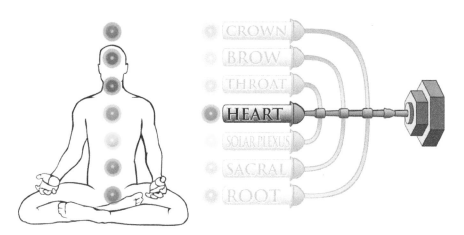

The heart chakra is indicated by the center mast of the menorah.
This is the point from which the chakras draw their power.

The menorah gives a picture of a manifold design, whereby the heart chakra connects and feeds the upper and lower chakras. This design gives the heart chakra influence and control over the whole system.

- The heart chakra is our most powerful center and great manager of the other chakras. This great center can bring us the greatest joy and can take us to depths of despair. The heart is our most precious center – the one of which we must take the greatest care.

- The heart is the great pump that propels life-sustaining blood, nutrition, and energy throughout our bodies.

- The heart chakra weighs all things. The heart chakra serves as our great scale, through which the issues of our life are weighed and measured.

- The heart chakra is more powerful than the sum of the lower chakras. Yet without understanding, the heart is subject to the unloving will of the lower chakras, creating an undesirable effect. We do better when we know better.

- The heart chakra is our spiritual core. From this center, we connect to others with love, compassion, and empathy.

The heart chakra is our emotional center. When we are emotionally strong, our bodies are strong. When our hearts are weak or hurting, we are weak and we hurt. The heart with all of its power is subject to pain and suffering. If we are to live a life filled with love, peace, and harmony, we must live by the laws of love.

May we take pause to consider the beauty of our unique design? Managing the body is like managing a three-ring circus.

Our lower ring of chakras drives us to seek survival, sex, pleasure, and power. (All good things when kept in balance.)

Our upper ring of chakras compels us to communicate, learn, create, and commune with the Divine.

Our great heart chakra is the ringleader, tasked with maintaining balance within the whole system. To do this effectively, it requires a greater force than the lower chakras, as well as control and understanding. The heart is not able to effectively take control of the body until joined with understanding and willpower from the mind.

The human body is a perfectly designed mechanism. It works amazingly well, even when we are unaware of what is going on. As we grow in awareness of the depth of our great potential, we will dream new dreams, and build a new love-filled world.

Love is at the heart of the matter.

THROAT/HEART/SOLAR PLEXUS CHAKRA CONNECTION

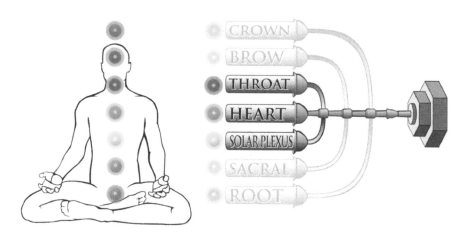

The throat / heart / solar plexus chakra connection is illustrated by the branch from the throat chakra, to the heart chakra, to the branch from the solar plexus.

This diagram illustrates the relationship between the solar plexus, heart, and throat chakra. While our power originates in the solar plexus, it is manifested through the throat chakra.

- Your voice is powered by air from your solar plexus. To feel this connection, push on your solar plexus, the area located just below your rib cage, and feel air rush from your throat.

- Our power does not come from our arms or our legs but from our ability to speak, sing, play music, hear, taste, touch, smell, and process information.

- As our consciousness is, our words express. When we are filled with intelligence, light, and love, then our words speak with understanding, light, and love. When we are filled with anger, jealousy, rage, deceit, or envy, then our words present ideas filled with such energy.

- From our voices comes the music of our souls. We express our inner light through the vibrational resonance of our words, songs, and music. As the heart is, so the mouth speaketh.

- Our great drive for power must be tempered by a greater drive for love, wisdom, and compassion so we might live together in peace as one family.

- The power of hearing. Our very survival often depends upon our ability to hear and perceive danger for our protection. We learn from what we hear.

- The throat chakra runs into the hands. This energetic connection gives us the great ability to express ourselves through the guitar, piano, and other great instruments. What is more important than our ability to play and to hear music or the sound of another's voice?

Our common objective in life should be to elevate our thoughts, attention, and energy into this higher center. It is from here we find our true ability to be an expression of love. For this reason, we should give careful thought to our words, and the energy we send with them. Our words project the intentions of our hearts and become the songs of our souls.

BROW/HEART/SACRAL CHAKRA CONNECTION

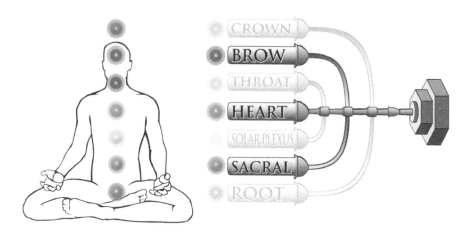

The brow / heart / sacral chakra connection is illustrated by the branch from the brow chakra, to the heart chakra, and then to the branch from the sacral chakra.

The brow chakra, aka "third eye chakra," empowers our great processing center and sixth sense. It is the mirror image of the medulla chakra, where Divine energy flows into the body. Mental concentration brings us automatically to this center, i.e., we involuntarily focus our eyes on this area when we think hard! Our intuition or sixth sense emanates from this center.

The brow, heart, sacral branch connection illustrates the dependent relationship between the two power centers. The sacral provides chi force energy to the brow chakra, and the brow chakra provides creative controls over our powerful drive for sex.

The mind is our supercomputer processor and requires a steady, reliable flow of energy to run the processes required for life. The synergy of energy developed in the human chakra system begins in the heart chakra and is directed into the lower sex chakra, where it is then radiated into our upper chakras and back around, continually energizing the body centers with life-giving chi forces.

The mind is the creative center for the spirit. Life and all things are manifested as dreams. Our thoughts become words, words become actions, and actions manifest our reality. It is from our great minds that we are able to imagine our world operating from a framework of love-based principals.

Knowing what we know about the brow chakra, we should not allow our children and community to be seduced by the media and other marketing companies using sexual or violent images for personal profit. This sacred center should be managed for the greater good of humanity.

Our life experience and reality are a product of what we have learned throughout our life. We should be mindful of the programming we allow to grow in the consciousness of our children, brothers, and sisters. That which we feed is what grows. We grow in light, by feeding the desires of our higher centers.

CROWN/HEART/ROOT CHAKRA CONNECTION

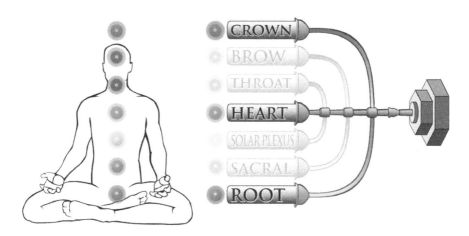

The crown / heart / root chakra connection is illustrated by the branch from the crown chakra, to the heart chakra, and then to the branch from the root chakra.

The crown chakra is our spiritual antenna. It is from this connection point that we communicate with the Divine. We send our thoughts and intentions into the universe, and we receive intuitive understanding from this high center.

- The crown, heart, root chakra connection gives us a picture of a complete electrical circuit. Divine light comes in through the crown chakra, into the heart chakra, where it is met with negative energy from the root chakra. This connection gives us our Divine spark.

- We are empowered by spiritual awareness. Our great purpose is to be an expression of our Divine nature. As we tune our attention to our truth, we are able to become the higher aspiration of our spirit selves.

- The condition of our mental health is relative to the condition of our spiritual health. When we walk in the truth of our higher selves, we walk with love, peace, joy, and a radiant power that brings health and vitality to our whole being. The power of thought is all consuming. In the light of wisdom and understanding, physical, mental, and spiritual alignments are healed, allowing one's essence to shine forth. Our nature is love, peace, health, and happiness. We only have to pluck the weeds of ill thought from our gardens to bear the wonderful fruit of our greater dreams.

- Earth school is a dynamic classroom where students create their own lesson plans by virtue of their thoughts and actions. As we focus our attention, thoughts, and actions on positive aspirations for life, we energetically pave the way for their manifestation.

All things are connected.
Whatever befalls the earth befalls the sons of the earth.
Man did not weave the web of life: he is only a strand in it.
Whatever he does to the web, he does to himself.

Chief Seattle, Nez Perce – 1854

LOWER CHAKRA SYSTEM
OUR PHYSICAL NATURE

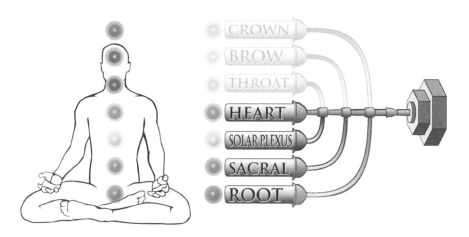

The lower chakra system is illustrated by the three lower
Branches connected to the center mast of the menorah.

Our lower chakra centers seek the lower pleasures relating to survival, sex, physical pleasure, and personal power. Because we live in the physical world, these physical desires have a command of our attention. While one drive center is powerful, the combined forces of the lower centers present a formidable force of reason to the body. Think about how much command your root chakra has over your mind when you are thirsty or hungry? The lower chakras seek the many forms of physical pleasure, comfort, and satisfaction. Survival related desires are there for a good reason of course, they just need to be managed.

We are able to better manage our lower centers once we have a conscious understanding of their presence, purpose, and function. Awareness changes everything. While the body may desire candy over a piece of broccoli, once you understand the benefits of the two, the broccoli looks a lot more appetizing.

UPPER CHAKRA SYSTEM
OUR SPIRITUAL NATURE

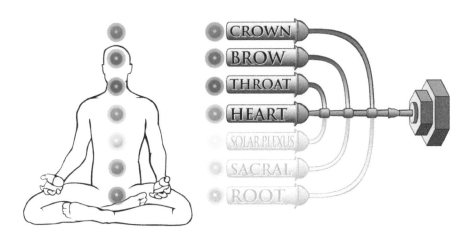

The upper chakra system is illustrated by the three upper branches attached to the center mast of the menorah.

The heart, throat, brow, and crown chakras are what make us rare creatures in this universe. These chakras combine to give us consciousness. All animal life has the ability to survive, to breathe, and procreate. We alone are given these higher functions. We alone have the responsibility to manage this world in a loving way.

The upper chakra system relates to the higher aspirations of our lives including:

- Our drive for love in all of her many forms
- Our drive to communicate, learn, speak, and to understand the nature of things
- Our drive to be creative; playing music, singing, dancing, painting, sculpting
- Our desire to care for Mother Nature
- Our desire to help others in life

- Our desire to learn about nutrition and medical healing for others
- Our desire to spend time in quiet, peaceful meditation
- Our desire to spend time with God
- Our desire to spend time with friends and loved ones
- Our desire to be an expression of our Divine selves

It is from here that we experience all the beauty that God and nature have to show us. It is from here that we co-create with God, building, manipulating, and caring for the natural world. With this tremendous gift comes the most serious responsibility. We are caretakers, who must balance what we take from this world, with the care we give.

PART THREE:
CHAKRAS ILLUSTRATED

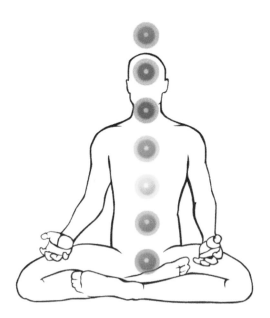

Chakras are a mysterious part of the human spiritual anatomy; yet without them, we would cease to exist. In an effort to bring about a greater clarity of chakras, I have assembled a small photo collage illustrating each chakra.

ROOT CHAKRA: DRIVE FOR SURVIVAL

Root Chakra - Drive for Survival. Is there anything we desire in life more than air to breathe, water to drink, food to eat, sleep for rest, and warmth? All of humanity shares a common drive for survival. When the basic needs of our survival are not met, we will do just about anything to meet them. The game of survival can be ugly and innocent people often get hurt. As an intelligent society, we must acknowledge our common need for survival. If God designed us to behave in a certain way, given a life condition, and we respond in that way, who are we to punish another for the behavior?

We live in a world of abundance. There is plenty to go around. If we are in fact human-spiritual beings here on Earth for the purpose of love, inner-personal growth, and to be an expression of our Divine nature, then the producing and sharing of food, sustenance, health care, and education becomes a mutual objective for all of humanity.

May we join together as a community with a common goal to provide the basic necessities of life for all of those in our community. As one grows in light, we all grow in light. As one suffers, we all suffer.

SACRAL CHAKRA:
DRIVE FOR SEX AND PLEASURE

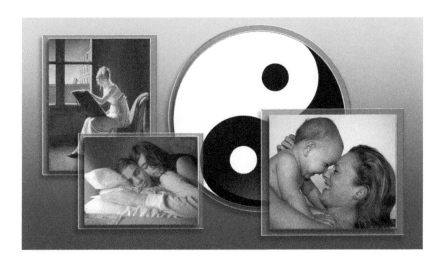

Sacral Chakra - Drive for Sex and Pleasure. The images above illustrate our natural desire for creative expression, intimate relations, procreation, and balance.

We are often driven by our desire for sex and pleasure. How much attention and energy does the average person spend in this center? Sexual energy feeds the senses, giving us pleasure. When the mind is sexually stimulated, we feel energized and active. Attachment to this energy can feel like a drug. Like-energy attracts like-energy. While powerful chi forces are good for us, these forces must be managed by our logical, thinking mind. *Reason, think, and then act.*

It is for, this reason, we should be cautious of alcohol and other drugs that cloud our thinking. An evening of sexual relations can change the course of our lives, forever. If we are going to change our destinies, may we do so with a higher creative purpose in mind?

What we feed is what grows. Finding balance with this center can be a challenge for every person. We manage this center by not feeding it with naughty imagery, and allowing our imaginations to fantasize. If we are to evolve as a community into a higher consciousness, may we consciously choose to live in the higher realms of thinking. As good teachers, it is good for us to make rules and set boundaries whereby we honor one another as the pure and holy people we truly are. Our bodies are the temples of the soul. If we are to walk in love, we must be able to justify our actions to our friends and family in the light of day. In our pursuit of perfection, may we live to a higher standard of love, based on the greater love we hold for ourselves.

SOLAR PLEXUS:
DRIVE FOR POWER

When it comes to money, how much is enough?
"Just a little bit more."

John Rockefeller

Solar Plexus - Drive for Power. Built into our programming is a natural drive to maintain our personal power. This natural drive compels us to protect the assets we have gathered for our survival. The images above illustrate our desire for shelter, money, success, and social status. While we all need a measure of power, this drive can compel us to unnecessary greed, and to hoard more than we reasonably need to survive. This drive is responsible for much of the pain and suffering we face today. While it is important that we live in a safe environment, it is through faith that we are able to keep this drive in check. People do terrible things to one another out of fear of losing power.

Fear and doubt drive us to an unnecessary compulsion for money and power. Our natural drives are powerful! How good does it feel to have a bunch of money in our hands? How about the joy of driving a really nice car or the comfort of living in a cozy home with all of the supplies we need to live comfortably?

While a measure of power is good and necessary for all people, natural manifestations of man's drive for power are greed, gluttony, and tyranny. Managing this drive can be a challenge for all of us. As we feed our drive for power, our drive for more power grows.

As the heart chakra brings balance and harmony to the body, may we embody the consciousness of love with all things in our lives.

That which we seek is what we will find.

HEART CHAKRA: DRIVE FOR LOVE

Heart Chakra - Drive for Love. What is more important in life than to love and to be loved? Love is the greatest drive, and something we all share. Our desire for love is not by accident, but by design. We can now understand why our desire for love is so strong.

This most powerful drive can bring one the greatest joy, and it can also lead one into the pits of despair. Even the great heart is subject to the laws of love. When the drive for love combines with the drive for sex, without clarity of thought, we may find ourselves in emotional turmoil that can be devastating. We are emotional creatures. To live a happy, joy-filled life, we must know and live by the laws of love. Love walks in truth. To master life, we must master our hearts and love.

Knowing that we are here to love, and to be an expression of love, frees us to become more loving. Like farmers, we must tend the gentle soil around the heart with all diligence. It is from the heart that we sow seeds of love, which one day become the fields that sustain us.

The fullness of love is our great joy. We feel with our hearts, and when our hearts are good, we are good. Love is vitality. Love is energy. Love is a force. Love produces love.

Looking at our world, it is humbling to witness the love that surrounds us. Here we are, hudling through space on this beautiful planet of blue oceans and snowcapped mountains with majestic forests, filled with wonderful animals, birds, scented flowers, and the most fragile butterflies. Observing the grandeur of creation is almost more than one can bear.

One could surmise that we must all be very important... We must be greatly loved!

THROAT CHAKRA:
DRIVE FOR COMMUNICATION

"As the heart is, the mouth speaketh."

(Luke 6:45)

Throat Chakra - Drive for Communication. Our throat chakra has to do with our ability to hear, to speak, to sing, to play music, and to learn. It is from this high center that we are able to receive information, knowledge, and wisdom of all kinds, and transform it into something entirely new, and of our own unique creation.

Our throat chakra is our magical center of transformation. It is from here that our heart speaks. As we tune our hearts to love, we tune our voices, thoughts, and energy into love-filled, energy patterns. As we bless, so are we blessed. We exist here on Earth to be an expression of this magical center. Our great power lies within our ability to speak, to sing, to dance, to play music, and to share our inner truth with others.

The voice is a channel for the soul. The greatest expression we have to share is music from our souls. Our hands can play instruments that transcend and resonate with Divine consciousness. Our voice can be trained on thoughts of love, peace, kindness, hope, joy, and all of the good things in life.

The act of communication is a high art. If we are here to be an expression of this high center, then we should encourage our children and all people to sing, dance, and exercise this most important center. What is more joyful than singing, dancing, or both? What a great joy to know that we are here for the purpose of sharing our love through this high center.

Our great power is within our voices, not our arms or fists. Our voices become powerful tools of manifestation when we use them to communicate with others the great ideas and plans we have.

Through our words, we are a fount of all goodness or a cesspool of evil.
May we set our sights on the high-ways of love.

BROW CHAKRA: DRIVE FOR WISDOM

Brow Chakra - Drive for Wisdom. The sixth chakra is our *sixth sense* "third eye" and center of intuition. We are truly magical creations. With the use of our most amazing minds, we are able to survive the wilds of living on Earth, grow and evolve as a species, and commune with the Divine. The mind is an amazing, creative computer by which we are able to process vast amounts of information and produce dreams that crystallize into reality. We have the ability to manage the dual energies within our bodies for our creative use. We have the ability to evolve our imaginations based on new knowledge. Yet, with all of our inner activity, we have the capacity to find peace and joy through quiet meditation.

Life is a mental experience, and it is vitally important that we properly feed and care for our mental faculty. Every aspect of life is processed through our minds. Our minds are our most sacred instruments, yet are programmable. As spiritual beings, we are only able to conceive the dreams our minds might imagine. If we are programmed with limited beliefs, we will only manifest those beliefs. Knowledge, wisdom, and understanding of our true capabilities changes everything. Once we understand the nature of the physical body and the grand potential of our spirit selves, we can focus our attention on our greater dreams, hopes, and aspirations.

The lower chakras desire pleasures of the lower centers. It is only by the power of love, and the will of our all-knowing minds, that we are able to direct our attention away from the body, and to the high-ways of love. That which we feed grows. We change the world by focusing our attention on the higher aspirations of spirit. Once we find love, we will no longer tolerate the needless starvation of children, murder, incarceration, war, disease, and the other crimes of humanity.

CROWN CHAKRA: DRIVE FOR SPIRITUALITY

Crown Chakra - Drive for Spirituality. This energetic center drives us to connect with our creator and is one of the most amazing parts of our spiritual hardware. Imagine, we have the ability to connect with the greatest force in the universe in a split second, with a mere thought. "Mother Father God, thank you for my life. Thank you for my wonderful body, my health, my great intellect, for my love and compassion."

Talking with God is good. It's even better when we know that every thought, hope, dream, or aspiration we might have is known. God knows our deepest thoughts, our greatest hopes, and our greatest fears. May we take heart knowing that God knows everything, and be everything that God might hope to see in us. There is freedom knowing that there is no hiding. We have no secret place or secret thoughts. We are all here to grow in love. All of our lessons in life are to bring us into alignment with our true selves, which is love.

There are many ways to learn lessons. Some of them hurt, and some of them are painless. We grow through wisdom and knowledge, or through doubt and fear. We may choose to put a hand in the fire and feel the pain of burning skin, or we may choose to learn about fire, and the benefits of heat, and heat management. We each determine our own lesson plan with our actions. To learn with wisdom, we must devote time to education and study. Our lessons come with conscious decisions.

We are connected to God for a reason, and that reason is love and fellowship. It is amazing to consider that we are made with the ability to commune with the Divine, yet the choice to commune lies with us. Why would one not want to connect with God? Fear and doubt of the reality of God keeps us from opening our hearts and minds to our great creator. Fear no more. Let there be no doubt about it. I am, you are, we are all part of the Divine kingdom here on Earth. Go boldly and bravely my friend, into the heart of the Divine, with your thoughts, aspirations, and prayers of a greater expanding love. Know that love, and the wisdom of love, is the answer we have all been looking for.

PART FOUR

ChakraSynergy for
the Human Being

*We now know where to find our gravitational
point of center; it's in the heart!*

CHAKRASYNERGY CROP CIRCLE

COURTESY: APEX NEWS & PICTURES
THE SYMBOL WAS 370 FEET LONG

The ChakraSynergy symbol was reproduced from a crop circle found sculpted into a sea of barley beneath Windmill Hill near Devizes Wilts, UK May 25, 2009. The symbol features the seven chakras of the human body and what appears to be a schematic design of the human bio-energy system. Note the large energetic center of the heart chakra, and the energetic lines connecting the upper and lower chakras. The ChakraSynergy symbol provides us with a wealth of information about the nature of our human spiritual design that until now was beyond our ability to comprehend.

ChakraSynergy illustrates the framework of our inner design. Yin and yang energies are managed and brought into balance by the power of love from the heart chakra. We live and survive as a species due to the powerful design of the heart chakra.

This symbol is one of the most important symbols of our time. This gift of knowledge brings us a greater understanding of love. It is through knowledge and understanding of our inner design that we are able to reconcile the reality of our existence. We are the handiwork of an amazing designer. What an awesome gift to be able to view our inner blueprint.

CHAKRASYNERGY: A SYNERGY OF ENERGY FOR THE HUMAN BEING

ChakraSynergy - I have taken artistic liberty with the ChakraSynergy symbol by coloring the chakras, orbs, and energetic lines in their natural order of color. Looking at the symbol, one can see seven chakras operating within three spinning systems; the lower chakra system, the upper chakra system, and the large, all-encompassing, heart chakra center. While we each embody three powerful systems, the controlling force of the heart chakra brings unity, oneness, and equilibrium to the whole system.

From a position of perfect balance, we are able to control our body mechanism with mere thought. It is amazing to think that we are powered by a symphony of color-light energy, emanating from our heart chakras, and flowing into and around our upper and lower chakra system.

ChakraSynergy gives us a picture of the word synergy. Synergy is defined as *The working together of two or more energies when the result is greater than the sum of their individual effects or capabilities.*

Some notable features of ChakraSynergy:

- ChakraSynergy presents us with a harp-shaped symbol, featuring seven colors of the rainbow and seven notes of the music scale. This symbol illustrates the musical nature of the human spiritual design.
- The large heart chakra is the energetic core of the energy body.
- The sacral chakra is the rotational center of the lower chakras.
- The brow chakra is the rotational center of the upper chakras.
- Energy bands emanating from the heart chakra form a yin/yang design, indicating that energy from the heart chakra spins in a clockwise rotation, encapsulating the whole chakra system.
- The lower chakra (yang) design indicates a counter-clockwise rotation around the negative pole of the sacral chakra. The gravitational force of the lower center pulls chi force energy from the root and solar plexus chakra into the sacral chakra.
- The upper (yin) chakra design indicates a counter-clockwise rotation around the positive pole of the brow chakra. The gravitational force of the upper center pulls spirit energy from the throat and crown chakra into the brow chakra.
- The rainbow of color-light energy around the heart chakra will turn into white light as it spins. It is no wonder that we have such a great desire to be light and loving because we are literally made of light and love.

ChakraSynergy provides us with key insight as to how three, very different systems, often with conflicting wants and needs, might coexist in a healthy, harmonious, and beautiful way. We survive due to the great power and controlling force of the heart chakra. Without the overriding power of our heart chakra, animal passions of the body would overpower spirit's quest for love. We are only able to manifest the higher aspirations of our Divine "will" when the power of our love is greater than our love of power. Jimi Hendrix coined this beautiful thought.

"When the power of love overcomes the love of power the world will know peace."

-Jimi Hendrix

While our energy body is designed to bring balance and equilibrium to the whole system, we have no such structure for our government, companies, or cultural organizations. *What is needed today within our social structures is an organizational framework of design, with love as the energetic center, and controlling force of reason, needed to manage competing energies present within the whole system?*

ChakraSynergy gives us amazing insight into the size and power of the heart chakra, and it also gives us reason for hope. We are energized by the power of love!

THE POWER OF LOVE

"In essence, the body is not flesh, but energy. Bodily functions are sustained by cosmic energy entering the medulla oblongata and working through the different chakra centers. If this energy were removed, our physical bodies would cease to operate."

– Alex Jones, Seven Mansions of Color

The ChakraSynergy symbol illustrates the energetic power of the human spiritual body. As we grow in understanding of our human spiritual design, we are able to increase our radiant power through our conscious awareness and intention.

By virtue of our Divine connection, we are able to send energy (good or bad) to anybody or anything at any time. We do not need a cell phone or an Internet connection. We only need to think of them, feel the energy, and send it to them. We are energetically tied into the mainframe of cosmic consciousness. We can choose to be a radiant expression of love, or not. What we do with our energy is up to us.

Energy moves in a circular motion. With this information in mind, we are able to consciously manage the energy we receive by managing the energy we send. We hold the power of love within the intentions of our heart and soul.

Knowing how to operate your spiritual equipment changes everything. Each and every moment involves some conscious decision. Within each moment you can choose to support desires of the body or the desires of spirit. With practice, you can move energy within your chakra system at will. You do this with thought. Beginning at your root chakra, imagine your life threatened for a moment and that you have to fight someone. From there, think about the pleasure of sex, money, love, speaking, creating something, and then singing to God. With this exercise, your energy field just ascended the full spectrum of color. Musically, you just played a chord. As you move your energy, you transform your color. The choice is up to you.

You are probably quite aware of your physical abilities and how to make your muscles stronger, but what about your spiritual abilities? To refine your spiritual gifts and abilities, you must first become aware of what they are and what they look like. To do this, one must be able to differentiate between the primal needs/wants of the physical body and the higher aspirations of spirit.

- Our understanding shapes our awareness
- Our awareness shapes our attitude
- Our attitude shapes our emotions
- Our emotions shape our actions
- Our actions shape our reality

Environment is everything. It is only after we have provided for the basic needs of survival that we are able to focus our attention on the higher aspirations of life. It is hard to be joyful and energetic when one is dying of thirst. Our lower chakras are not bad; they are necessary for our survival. If we do not survive, we cannot ascend to our spiritual fullness! Lower chakras must be listened to, and their needs weighed.

Creative consciousness on demand – by virtue of our powerful heart chakra, the spirit has dominion over the body. With this ability, we are able to ascend into the higher wavelengths of consciousness at will. We have been blessed with a means for managing our lower forces so that we might be a creative expression of our Divine nature.

What we feed in life is what grows. We manage our primal passions by feeding them what they need, not all that they might want. This, of course, is the real challenge for almost everybody. Finding balance in the pursuit of pleasure and power requires a depth of reasoning, discipline, faith, and understanding of what is best for our lives.

The high-ways of love - Knowledge and understanding of one's whole self is the key to one's ascension into higher consciousness. Even though we are made of many dynamic parts, we are one creation. We consciously grow the higher aspirations of our Divine nature, by focusing our attention, education, exercise, practice, and money on the aspirations of our higher nature.

Some practical application – There are benefits to understanding the rules to the game and how things work. Through understanding our body and spirit connection with the Divine, we can project the desired outcome for a future event. For example: Before you attend the next social gathering, pray for the desired outcome of the event. You can pray for great conversation, hearts to be open, or learning, or whatever the outcome you desire. Your prayer of energy will fill the space with love before you arrive.

Love is in the air when we send it there.

Higher energy has a greater power to express light. We connect with the Divine on the very highest level of our energy. When we understand this and consciously connect in this way, we become in-tune with the will of the Divine.

PART FIVE

THE SCIENCE OF SPIRITUALITY

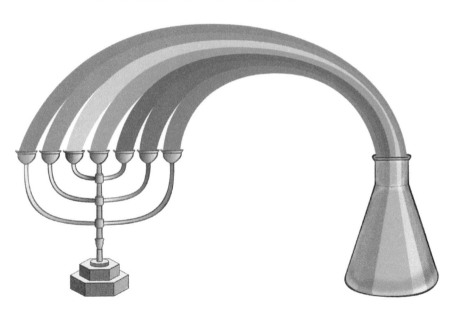

Mother Nature's Rainbow
Bridging Science and Spirituality

THE RAINBOW BRIDGE

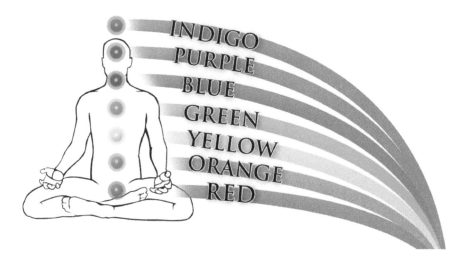

Who would have guessed that the rainbow would be the bridge that interlinks humankind with Mother Nature? Yet what a beautiful reminder we have of our Divine connection.

As you will note from the image above, the pattern of colors found in the rainbow, match, and interlink with the pattern of colors found in the human chakra system. What is significant for us here is the consistency of the pattern of colors we clearly see within the rainbow, the prism, and the chakra system. While the pattern of colors in the rainbow is readily visible for us to see, we do not normally see one another's chakras illuminated. (For information on this technology see Psy-Tek Subtle Energy Research Lab, at the back of the book.)

Mother Nature's Rainbow illustrates nature's natural law of harmony. We can see this harmony in the seamless transition of color from red, to orange, to yellow, to green, to blue, to indigo, to violet, and then into other octaves of color of greater or lesser range, beyond our ability to perceive. The colors are separate and yet they flow seamlessly into one another, creating a beauty far surpassing each individual layer. We can measure the energetic vibrations with electronic equipment designed to measure waves and frequencies, and we can hear the harmony played out in the music scale. Nature's science presents a spectacle of color, light, and energy that we can see, hear, and feel.

Light is actually a living intelligence that we can see within the rainbow. We exist as a manifestation of this light.

The pattern of colors within Mother Nature's rainbow provides us with her organizational framework of design. Her design illustrates a *harmoniously integrated system*, of color-light energy, of which we are able to detect a small segment with our eyes. In the radiant energy spectrum, we are able to see the portion between the infrared and ultraviolet rays. Like a chord of music on the piano, we are able to see a chord of light in the energy spectrum.

To live in harmony with Mother Nature, we simply use Mother Nature's framework of design as a model for designing the many physical systems and social structures within our world. Such systems would bring us in tune with Mother Nature's many layers of systems. Balance and harmony with nature are the ultimate objective and great challenge for humankind. Peace and harmony follow love. We will bring harmony into the world when we bring our relationships, social structures, and governments into harmony with Mother Nature through her pattern of design. Mother Nature's grand architecture gives us a model for life, and reason for hope. We now have the framework of design needed to build heaven, right here on Earth.

The theory of random evolution no longer stands as a theory of any merit. Standard modern thought on evolution understands creation to be a meaningless tangle of elements affecting each other, all simply striving for survival. A higher form of evolution is described as emergence. This planet, our solar system, each person, and all of nature are the emerging product of Divine thought and creation. We are surrounded by physical evidence of Divine creation. From the tiniest atom to the grandest galaxy in our universe, the rainbow pattern of color-light energy can be seen everywhere. Divine consciousness and love are forever evolving, forever new.

We are not a product of some random accident. We are part of Divine creation as is all of Mother Nature. We are here for a purpose, and that purpose is love. We, like all things alive, are emerging. Our lives have meaning and purpose, and we are called as one to emerge into the loving, gentle creation that has been evolving from the beginning of time.

Emerge therefore in love and with confidence, knowing that the sweet radiance of love is at hand.

Let the rainbow be our guide and unifying principle,
which illuminates our path to love.

THE PRISM CONNECTION

White light shining into a prism naturally divides into individual wavelengths of color-light energy. These colors match the color pattern in the rainbow and the human chakra system. This fact provides us with another omen, telling us of our energetic connection to Mother Nature.

White light is the sum of all colors combined.

As a prism naturally divides white light into its seven component colors, so does Divine energy magically divide into the full spectrum of colors as it enters our crown chakra from where it is distributed throughout our chakra system.

Mother Nature's natural order of color, light, and energy is a foundational truth which leads us to greater peace and harmony.

Taking our cue from Mother Nature, we now have a holistic way to organize the matters of our lives into Mother Nature's Organizational Framework of Design.

THE MUSIC OF CHAKRAS

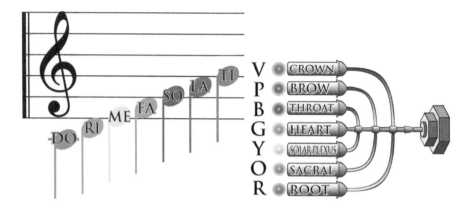

> *"Each note on the musical scale has a corresponding color and every color has a corresponding note. Sound and color are the same thing, perceived by different senses. It is a perception of vibration."*

–Alex Jones, Seven Mansions of Color

As human spiritual beings, we are a symphony of color, light, and energy. Within each chakra system we see an ascending scale of music as in do, re, me, fa, so, la, ti and a descending scale of music. In my research, I found the pattern of seven to be one of the most significant and surprising findings. How basic is the relationship between the scale of music, the rainbow, the prism, and our chakra system? Imagine teaching a child to connect color and music. What fun that would be! To paint music! To see and hear color!

The ChakraKey illustrates the fundamentals of color-light energy that power our body. Each color has a vibrational resonance, a musical tone, and a color energy pattern. When we are in tune, our energy is full and we are bright. When we are out-of-tune, our flame flickers and we are weak.

Middle C is red, D is orange, E is yellow, F is green, G is blue, A is indigo, and B is violet. The note F is the sound of love and green is her color...

and here we go again, patterns that underlie sound, coming in layers of seven. The seven-candle menorah, the seven major colors of the rainbow, the seven chakras, and now the seven-note scale.

As musical beings, we brighten when listening to music with uplifting harmonies. When we listen to dark, heavy music, our energy becomes depressed and primal.

Mothers, teach your children to play music. We develop genius in our children when we teach them to read and play music. Music is the high art of creativity.

You can hear the music of the rainbow. With a xylophone, piano, or guitar, play the color/note of each rainbow color. This is the sound of Mother Nature's harmony.

Listen. Can you hear it? The music. I can hear it everywhere.
In the wind ... in the air... in the light. It's all around us.
All you have to do is open yourself up.
All you have to do ... is listen.

– August Rush

THE NATURE OF COLOR

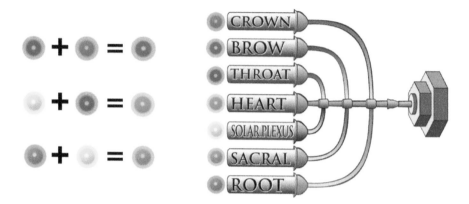

Looking to the colors on the ChakraKey, note how they naturally combine to make the complementary color.

- Red and yellow energy from our lower chakras, spin in a counter-clockwise direction, producing the orange energy.

- Blue and violet energy from our upper chakras, spin in a counter-clockwise direction, producing the indigo energy center.

- Yellow energy from the lower chakras and blue energy from the upper chakras are brought together in a clockwise rotation, creating the powerful green vibration of the heart chakra.

The Color of Love - The human aura can take on different colors depending on one's physical surroundings, emotional state, and consciousness. In survival mode, one's energy is red, orange, or yellow. While safely walking through a lush valley of green grass and foliage, one's energy and aura would move into the colors green and blue. We ascend into our higher energies only after we have secured the items needed for survival, and we are safe among friends. Energetically, we are the color of our consciousness.

"The soul is dyed the color of its thoughts. Think only on those things that are in line with your principles and can bear the full light of day. The content of your character is your choice. Day by day, what you choose, what you think, and what you do is who you become. Your integrity is your destiny...it is the light that guides your way."

– Heraclitus (540-480 B.C.)

Heraclitus must have been a very wise man to know that our souls are dyed the color of our thoughts. The images above give us reason to consider the color of energy we are radiating because all energy is circular. The color we radiate is the color we receive; somehow, someway.

Ultimately, we are a radiant source of color-light energy. As we choose to live in the higher frequencies of love, we become a radiant source of green, blue, indigo, and violet-colored energy.

As energetic beings, we are able to detect many forms of energy with our most amazing body mechanism.

- We can see light with our eyes
- We can hear sound with our ears
- We can smell with our noses
- We can taste with our mouths
- We can see and hear vibrational waves of energy with our eyes and ears
- We can sense one another's vibrational energy with our spirits
- We can feel our inner energy as good or bad, weak or strong
- We can measure electric energy with our hands and electronic equipment
- We can feel hot or cold energy with our bodies

We are able to generate different kinds of energy; all born of thought.

Our thoughts directly affect our energy. Where our thoughts go, our energy flows. As we master our thoughts and energy, we change the radiant color of our energy field from red to orange, to yellow, to green, to blue, to purple, to violet, or white light. As we grow in knowledge and control of our body mechanisms, we grow in control of our personal light. Through understanding the nature of our energy, we are able to master our inner light and rise at will, into the higher vibrations of color. This mastery is called enlightenment. In-Light-en-ment!

What color are you? Conscious awareness of your emotional condition makes all of the difference. When feeling down, raise your energy with thoughts of thanks and gratitude for your health, family, and the very gift of life itself.

As a consciously-aware, human spiritual being, you hold the power of love within your thoughts and intentions. With your desire, you become a conduit for Divine love to flow through you, to any place you wish. If we think it, and we want it, we can become a powerful force of loving intention.

We are more than what we may seem; we are an evolving dream.

THE NATURE OF ENERGY

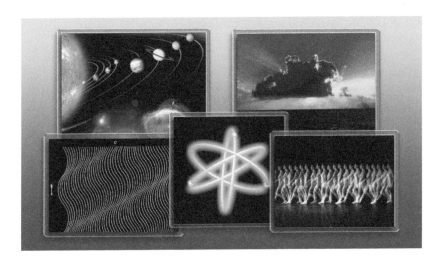

"Everything is energy and that's all there is to it.
Match the frequency of the reality you want and you cannot help
but get that reality. It can be no other way. This is not philosophy.
This is physics."

- Albert Einstein

The images above illustrate the rotational nature of energy. From the tiniest atom to the grandest galaxy in the heavens, energy moves in a circular motion. We can observe these phenomena in the sound we hear, the light we see, and on a grand scale, by observing the planets within our solar system revolve around the sun.

As a spiritual being, you are a powerhouse of invisible, spirit-light energy. You are so energetically powerful, you can say, "I love this water," or "I hate this water." One thought will bring health and vitality to the water, and one thought will bring sickness and poison. Your thoughts carry a powerful force into the universe that will affect you or others in some positive or negative way. Awareness of your energetic capability will change your life, and possibly the world.

The great lesson for us here is that our power is not in our physical might, but in the radiant energy within our emotions. The energy we possess and radiate is like all other forms of energy within nature; it's circular. The energy we send around comes around.

We manage our energy with our thoughts:

- Where your attention goes, your energy flows
- Manage your attention, manage your energy
- Manage your energy, manage your dreams
- Manage your dreams, manage your life

The choice is up to you. You have the power to choose positive thoughts and ideas that bring positive energy into your life, or you can choose negative thoughts that draw negative energy into your reality.

We are made to love and to manifest all that goes with being an expression of Divine consciousness. As you consciously direct your energies into a greater creative expression of love, you will become more loving and attract more love.

Each chakra carries a unique, resonate vibration, color, sound, intelligence, and energy that we can feel. Awareness of one's energy is necessary to master oneself.

- Crown - Energy of prayer & meditation
- Brow – Creative-thought energy
- Throat - Vocal and music vibration
- Heart – Energy of love, peace, and contentment
- Solar Plexus – Energy of social power and money
- Sacral – Sexual energy
- Root – Survival-based energy

We are created to be gentle, loving people. We are here on Earth to be an expression of our creative consciousness, which is love. To prove this point, try this exercise. Think about something you find boring or are not particularly fond of doing. How does your heart feel? Does it feel open and full, or closed? Now think about something that really inspires you – what do you love to do? Feel your heart energy again; is it full and vibrant? Hold on to the inner awareness of how you feel when you are involved with inspired thought and actions. Our goal and purpose in life are to be involved with activity that inspires us and fills us with light. This is who we are made to be; this is our integrity. Simple as it might seem, living a life of integrity involves "following your bliss."

When we perceive life from our higher chakras, we are able to contemplate the higher aspects of our spirit nature. When we perceive the desires of our lower chakras, we are limited to primal ideas. This has been our way of thinking for thousands of years. The evolution of thought is our great challenge today. When our thoughts are based upon survival, or solely on the pursuit of pleasure and power, the outcome may or may not show any regard for the human condition. As long as the pursuit of money and power is our greatest objective in life, we will forever live in a world with war, violence, and despair.

We change the negative forces in our world by not feeding them with our attention, our money, and our support. We build a more loving world by feeding ideas, programs, and social structures that support education, high ideals, and love. When our thoughts and energy are motivated by love, we will manifest a loving outcome.

We change our world by understanding the big picture and holding fast to our greater integrity as kind, loving, compassionate human beings.

As sons and daughters of light, we have the right!

- Claim your right to be the expression of light God made you to be
- Claim your personal integrity
- Claim your power with your voice

As you move into the direction of your higher purpose, you will feel a shift in consciousness. The winds of purpose and intention will fill your sails with new energy, love, and power. The chains that held you from moving forward will be broken, and a new light will fill your life. Seek love, my friend. You owe it to yourself, to the many that came before you, and to the many still to come, to be the greatest expression of radiant light and love that you might become.

Your objective is to become the most loving version of yourself possible. If you are a painter, then paint, with the greatest ability you might express. If you are inspired to build, then build. If you are a mother – love, watch over, and teach your children well. We have so many options for our lives. With each day comes a new opportunity, to be the inspired expression of love that lies within us.

Exercise your Power of love - Your great power is found within your heart, your voice, your mind, and your connection with divine consciousness. You exercise this power by sending your ideas, thoughts, and desires to others through your connection with Divine consciousness, with hearts filled with thanks and gratitude for the desired outcome. There is a science to prayer. The energy and vibration you send out will return to you in some magical way.

Like energy produces like energy. There can be no other way…

THE PARABLE OF THE FLEA CIRCUS

Fleas have the natural ability to jump three to four feet into the air. In preparation for training fleas for a flea circus, one only has to put fleas into a cake dish with a clear glass top for a few days. When the fleas first arrive, they continually jump and bump their heads on the glass ceiling. After a few days of hitting their heads, the fleas learn to jump just below the height of the ceiling. At this point, the trainer can remove the lid, and the fleas will jump no higher than their training will allow.

In many ways we are much like the fleas; limited by past experience. We are unaware of the great potential we possess. We have been trained to live in small, controlled ways when in fact, we are supernatural, human/spiritual beings connected to Divine consciousness and capable of unimaginable feats. Once we recognize our true nature and figure out how to manage our energy, look out! Things will change once we know what change should look like.

I invite you to take hold of your power. Imagine that you could do anything, what would you do?

- How high can you jump?
- How big can you dream?
- How much can you love?
- How much do you care?
- What might you create?
- What light might you shine?
- What kind of intelligent force can you bring to the cause of love?

You grow in power and light with each moment you maintain conscious awareness of the light. You will become what you desire.

Desire what you love and swim in this ocean. As a Divinely-inspired human spiritual being, you are a force of love. It is time to release the great light of love that lives within you. It is time to soar on wings of love.

"It's not how much we give, but how much love we put into giving."

- Mother Teresa

"Ask, and it shall be given to you; seek and ye shall find; knock, and it shall be opened unto you."

Matthew 7.7

THE NATURE OF DUAL FORCES

Yin and Yang Symbol

The yin/yang symbolizes the dual nature of all things. Every aspect, person, and event has both a dark side and a light side. Each side contains a measure of the other's substance; the symbol represents the interconnectivity between the two. They exist together.

Duality – the state of being twofold: Existence divided equally between opposing attributes; necessary opposites (one side balances the other.)

Did you ever stop to think about the duality of nature? The yin and yang of life is all around us. We are each a human animal and a spirit being – two creatures bound within one body. Both dynamic entities seek to rule the one. It is good to have an awareness of the dual nature of life. The more we grasp the idea and reasoning behind the nature of duality, the more we are able to see the genius within the structure.

Some observations about the value of duality:

- Polarity is a natural law
- Dual energies are necessary components of creation
- Yang is the male force, and yin represents the female force of creation

We need not fear duality, but we must learn to find a balance between the two sides of our nature. In the world of duality, understanding the nature of dual energies is required to master the energy.

The Law of Relativity is present everywhere in creation:

yin/yang	life/death	hot/cold
black/white	wet/dry	light/dark
night/day	love/hate	good/bad
fast/slow	soft/hard	sweet/bitter
truth/lie	body/spirit	man/woman
on/off	fire/ice	young/old
order/chaos	giving/receiving	clear/solid
clarity/confusion	smooth/rough	passive/active
mother/father	winter/summer	health/disease
intuition/logic	North/South pole	attract/repel
internal/external	positive/negative	kind/mean
pleasure/pain	heaven/hell	inside/outside
plus/minus	liquid/solid	ebb/flow
feminine/masculine		

Taoism uses the yin/yang symbol to represent the need for two forces to come together in the act of creation. Two forces coming together with equal force can result in an ongoing battle for the will of one or the other.

ChakraSynergy gives us a diagram of the human spiritual design. While we are made of both yin and yang energy, we live, survive, and thrive because of the over-riding power of the heart chakra. Lower Yang energy is of the body, and the upper yin energy is of spirit. Yang energy is strong and would overpower our yin energy if not for the balancing power of our heart chakra. Our heart chakra is able to harness the power of yang energy for the creative use of our greater selves.

If you think about it, everything requires mastery. The very act of standing takes quite a bit of mastery. Finding balance in all the positions we might assume would keep a computer busy for days. Finding the most desirable temperature for the room can require mastery. A desirable room temperature might depend upon what one finds to be comfortable. It might depend upon the ambient temperature outdoors. It might depend upon how much heat or air conditioning one can afford. Finding balance with the simplest issues we face can be a daunting task.

Mastery is the key to living a balanced life. To master something, we must know everything about it. Mastery takes practice, understanding, knowledge, and more practice. We face untold decisions within our lives every day. We are forever making perfect decisions, and we are forever making small errors. It is in our nature to find the errors and make corrections great and small. We are wonderfully made to master our world. It is our duty, honor, and obligation to master our lower selves so we might spend our time and attention mastering the greater gifts we have to share. We find balance, peace, and harmony when we bring the issues of life through the heart.

If we are to evolve in a loving way here on Earth, love must be the engine that motivates our actions.

We are the greatest expression of the Divine here on Earth. Our emerging evolution is up to us. Divine love comes with the freedom to say yes or no. It is up to us to be mindful of clues left for us that we might consciously evolve in a loving way here on Earth.

Together, we must acknowledge our human spiritual design.

- Our drive for survival is given and should be understood
- Our drive for sex is given and should be managed
- Our drive for power is given and should be managed
- Our great drive for love is given and should be encouraged
- Our drive for communication is given and should be encouraged
- Our drive for wisdom is given and should be encouraged
- Our drive for God is given and should be encouraged

We share a common purpose of elevating the life conditions of humanity into the higher aspiration of love. We will only accomplish this when our motives and our intentions join together for this purpose.

Love is a conscious choice.

PART SIX

The Nature of Love

*Love is the merging of two lives, two hearts,
and two souls, into a new and greater light.*

WHAT IS LOVE?

What is love? That is the question...

While there are many uses of the word love, this book is dedicated to a higher view of this most important word. If love is to be the foundational idea for our world, then we should gather around a definition that will stand with integrity.

"Love is an emotion of a strong affection and personal attachment. Love is also a virtue representing all of human kindness, compassion, and affection; and the unselfish, loyal, and benevolent concern for the good of another. Love may also be described as actions towards others, or oneself, based on compassion, or as actions towards others, based on affection."– Wikipedia

Given Wikipedia's definition of love, we can begin to understand the many aspects of love.

Love is an emotion. Our emotions are the inner gauges we use to measure our energy as positive or negative, happy or sad, love or hate, joy or sorrow, peace or chaos.

Love is a strong affection. The term strong affection refers to a strong sense of positive energy.

Love is of personal attachment. While is love is of personal attachment, love transcends all things, and makes room for one another to follow one's greater purpose.

In essence, love is a positive flow of energy that feels good.

Love is a virtue, representing all of human kindness and compassion. As our energy rises into our higher selves; we are compelled to be a greater expression of love through our loving actions. Conversely, when we feel unloved, unlovable, sad, remorseful, guilty, depressed, unhappy, suppressed, enslaved, caged, or a wide range of negative emotions, our energy drops into our lower centers.

Negative energy does not feel so good.

- Primal feelings and energy reside in our lower chakras.
- Primal actions are out-of-tune with our inner peace and harmony.
- Unloving actions left unresolved lead to dis-ease.
- Dis-ease leads to death

In essence, love is emotional energy that we can feel, measure and see as color; such as red with anger, orange with passion, yellow with desire, green with love, blue with harmony, indigo with inspiration, and violet with bliss. With each color, there is a corresponding wavelength of energy and frequency. We are empowered with awareness of our different emotional states. If we are aware of how we feel about someone or something, and we wish to bring greater joy or energy to the moment, we only have to think of the condition with higher thoughts. We are emotional creatures. When we are emotionally in-tune, we are happy, content, and productive. Misplaced emotions can lead to disharmony, dis-ease, stress, misunderstanding, and fear.

Emotional intelligence – As we grow in understanding of our chakra centers, and the emotions associated with each chakra, we grow in emotional intelligence and resilience. As we expand our inner knowledge of things, we are able to emotionally rationalize how and why we feel the way we feel. The benefit of understanding one's emotions is enormous. Through growing in emotional intelligence, we are able to:

- Grow in self-awareness
- Grow in social awareness
- Transform our lives and relationships

- Improve physical health by reducing stress
- Improve every aspect of our lives

Either we rule our emotions, or our emotions rule us. Knowledge and wisdom of our spiritual equipment make all the difference. Love feels good. A choice for love is a choice for higher energy and brighter light. Higher energy will attract higher energy. Love produces love.

Our perspective about our purpose in life changes everything. While it is important that we honor our lower drives, as they are there to serve us, we do not live to serve them.

We are here in Earth school to learn, to teach, to help others, to love, to care, to create, to build, to sing, to dance, and to be an expression of the light that God gave us to shine. We are here to live in the higher realms of consciousness.

THE HIERARCHY OF LOVE

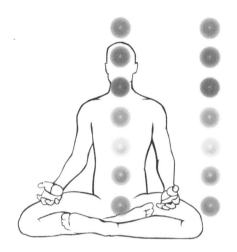

CROWN CHAKRA

BROW CHAKRA

THROAT CHAKRA

HEART CHAKRA

SOLAR PLEXUS CHAKRA

SACRAL CHAKRA

ROOT CHAKRA

The chart above illustrates the hierarchy of our human spiritual design. We are complex creatures with complex bodies and emotions. To best manage the many physical and emotional matters of life, our creator divided our spirit energy throughout our body in a hierarchy of seven energetic centers. The pattern of colors within the rainbow gives us a picture of the graduated frequencies of color-light energy within our chakra system, beginning with our red root chakra extending up through the violet crown chakra. Different energies are required for different aspects of our lives.

For instance, we can tell the difference between our feelings about pizza and how we feel about a loved one; with the difference being that of vibration and intensity. With awareness of our inner gauges, we can put our feelings for food in the root chakra, and our feelings for a loved one in our heart chakra. It is important for one to have an awareness of each energy center, to keep emotions in proper harmony with the body. We are only able to do this with an understanding of our inner construction. Within the hierarchy of our design is a logic we must bow to. We are designed to respond a variety of life conditions in a way that might bring us pleasure while ensuring our survival.

- We have been blessed with amazing bodies able to survive the wilds of living here on Earth.

- We have been given the pleasure of sexual relations, that we might produce many homes for other spiritual beings to live in.

- We are given a natural drive to obtain the resources we need for our survival.

- With our powerful heart center, we are designed to bring love, compassion, equilibrium, and balance into our many creations here on Earth.

- With our wonderful ability to speak, sing, play music, learn, and to process information, we are made to be wonderful performers on the stage of life.

- With our wonderful creative, intuitive sense of being, we are made with a genius ability to create forms and ideas of our wildest imagination.

- With our connection with the Divine, we are made to be in tune with all of conscious creation.

We are holy made to be an expression of love here on Earth. May we recognize our great design and take advantage of all of our wonderful features.

THE GOLDEN RULE

The Golden Rule, our common ground for love, peace, and prosperity.

Muslims, Jews, and Christians share a very sacred piece of common ground. That ground is called "The Golden Rule." The Golden Rule admonishes us to, "Do unto others, as we would have others do unto us." This simple idea is fundamental to all religions. The words are crafted a little differently, but the meaning is largely the same.

The Golden Rule is a simple precept that when followed, has the power to unite people of all colors and religions in the name of love. The things we do, "our actions," are born of our thoughts and intentions. When our intentions are filled with love, then we present loving intentions and actions to our friends. Our relationships grow when we honor one another with our loving thoughts and actions.

When our intentions are filled with jealousy, hate, envy, lust, or revenge, then our actions reflect this inner state, and we react with anger, fear, and violence. We suffer, as well as those we hurt.

Christ compels us to love with a commandment; the only one he gave us.

"A new commandment I give unto you, that ye love one another; as I have loved you, that ye also love one another." John 13:34 (King James Version)

Live by the Golden Rule. Treat others as you would want to be treated. The practice of reciprocity is a central tenet of Christianity.

In the Sermon on the Mount, Jesus teaches: *"So in everything, do to others what you would have them do to you, for this sums up the Law and the Prophets."* Matthew 7:12 (New International Version)

The Apostle Paul weaves the Golden Rule into the fabric of the church.

The entire law is summed up in a single command: "Love your neighbor as yourself." Galatians 5:14 (New International Version)

Learn to trust that love is stronger than hate. While we cannot control what other people do, we can control our energy. When we practice unconditional love, we become a force of love. Jesus teaches that we should love our enemies. The spiritual journey is the day-by-day practice of loving in the face of fear, hatred, bigotry, prejudice, and evil.

Unconditional love allows energy to flow naturally and abundantly between human beings. If there are no conditions, no requirements, and no demands, then we are free to be honest and to allow the power of love to flow through us. We are not afraid.

Love is the power that allows us to forgive others.

Then Peter came to Jesus and asked, *"Lord, how many times shall I forgive my brother when he sins against me? Up to seven times?"* Jesus answered, *"I tell you, not seven times, but seventy-seven times."* Matthew 18:21-22 (New International Version)

If we practice being loving, we will have the ability to forgive seventy-seven times over.

Love is compassion as compassion is love. As a most capable and intelligent group of friends, may we be observant to the most basic needs of the less educated and less fortunate people of Earth, and help them to elevate their life condition as needed.

"For I was hungry, and you gave me something to eat, I was thirsty, and you gave me something to drink, I was a stranger and you invited me in, I needed clothes, and you clothed me, I was sick and you looked after me, I was in prison and you came to visit me. Then the righteous will answer him, 'Lord, when did we see you hungry and feed you, or thirsty and give you something to drink? When did we see you a stranger and invite you in, or needing clothes and clothe you? When did we see you sick or in prison and go to visit you?" The King will reply, *'Truly I tell you, whatever you did for one of the least of these brothers and sisters of mine, you did for me."* - Matthew 25:35-40 (New International Version)

We harness the power of love with our loving intentions:

- Love-filled intentions flow into loving-filled actions
- Love-filled actions return love-filled reactions.
- The life we perceive is the life we will receive.

The law of reciprocity states:

- Love is the law, and the law is love
- Love produces love
- Kindness produces kindness
- Anger produces anger
- Bitterness produces bitterness
- Goodness produces goodness

"The love we take is equal to the love we make."

- The Beatles

WHAT LOVE IS NOT

While love is many things, there are many things not born of loving thoughts, resulting in energy and actions not born of love. Unfortunately, there are many things we can point to in our world today not born of love, such as acts of greed, lust, envy, revenge, hate, fear, war, revenge, and the raw pursuit of power. What love is not, gives us perspective on what love is… The choice is ours.

Below is a partial list of what love is not:

- Love is not lying
- Love is not stealing
- Love is not cheating
- Love is not lust
- Love is not envy
- Love is not mean
- Love is not a trick
- Love is not hurt
- Love is not murder
- Love is not boiling in anger
- Love is not rushing to judgment
- Love is not seeking revenge
- Love is not gluttony
- Love is not prideful
- Love is not sex
- Love is not impatient
- Love is not greedy
- Love is not self-pity or sloth

- Love is not cruel
- Love is not painful
- Love is not indifferent
- Love is not conspiring to do mean things
- Love is not withholding love out of spite
- Love is not lashing out in anger
- Love is not rooted in negative thought
- Love is not causing harm to others

To master the light and the darkness, one must understand both. As wise students, we do better when we know better.

THE VIRTUES OF LOVE

While love is ultimately indefinable, there are many things we can agree that love is. Below is a list of some of the essential virtues of love. The rules of love are written into our DNA. Ultimately we can feel that which is loving and that which is not. As we grow in wisdom of love, our emotional compass keeps us aligned with our greater integrity, and directs us deeper into the heart of love.

What is Love?

♥ Love is kind. Kindness is love. Kindness is an active expression of love. When we are kind, we are love.

♥ Love is caring, sharing, and being a friend. Love is reaching out to friends and those in need. When we take the time and effort to help someone in all of the many ways we are able – that is love.

♥ Love is adoring. To adore someone is to truly love them unconditionally.

♥ Love is forgiving. Forgiveness is love and a powerful form of energetic healing.

♥ Love is gratitude. Gratitude is love. When gratitude flows within us, the energy of thanks and appreciation flows. Love rests in gratitude.

♥ Love is patient. Patience is love. As love is a force, love is resistance. Love is when we give pause, hold, slow down, or wait for someone patiently.

♥ Love is compassion. Compassion is love. Our acts of compassion provide a conduit for the power of love to flow through us and into another.

♥ Love is empathy. As we love another, we are able to understand another's situation, feelings, and motives.

♥ Love is joy. Joy is love. What better emotion can we feel than joy? Joy lives in love, peace, and contentment.

♥ Love is enlightenment. When we are enlightened, we have discovered the truth of who we are as spiritual beings. Living in love is living in light.

♥ Love is eternal. Love transcends time, space, and matter.

♥ Love is giving. When we give, we love. When our giving begins with heartfelt intentions, our giving sets a force into motion that returns to us in ways beyond our imagination.

♥ Love is balance. Love weighs all things. Love is harmony. Love is perfect. Love transcends all things to find perfection.

♥ Love is harmony. Love is a vibration filled with perfect harmony.

♥ Love is truth. Love is truth and filled with light. Deceit is filled with darkness and negative energy. Negative produces negative. Light produces light.

♥ Love is free. Love comes with a creative choice: To give or not to give. To love or not to love. To accept or to reject.

♥ Love is knowledge. To love is to know. To know is to possess knowledge of a subject. To master oneself, one must be aware of their spiritual nature.

♥ Love is creative. Creative expression is love. Love is all that is beautiful, all that is lovely, all that is pure, all that is true, all that is of Divine expression that emanates from within nature.

♥ Love is careful. When we are careful, we are full of care; love is full of care.

♥ Love is light. Light is love. Love is a vibration of energy that emits a radiant light.

♥ Love is affluent. When our love is affluent, there is a great flow of giving and receiving the positive energies of love.

♥ Love is peace. Peace is love. When we at peace we are in a state of love. When we are in love, we are in a state of peace.

♥ Love is mercy. Mercy is love. Often we learn by making mistakes. When we show mercy to one another, we give one another permission to fail. Failing is part of learning.

♥ Love is hope. Hope is love. Our hopes contain our dreams and imaginations for the visions we see coming to light.

♥ Love is faith. Faith is love. Faith rests in certainty knowing that we are love.

♥ Love is good. Goodness is love. Good is desirable.

♥ Love is priceless. How can we put a value on love? What is more important?

♥ Love is selfless. When we are selfless, we are generous, noble, and gallant.

♥ Love is openness. When we are open, we are transparent and honest.

♥ Love is charity. Charity is love. Giving to those in need is love in action. When you give, give knowing that your sharing is the watering of a beautiful soul.

♥ Love is secure. When we are secure, we have faith in knowing that we are safe and secure in love.

♥ Love is safe. When we are safe, we are able to grow in love.

♥ Love is generous. Our generosity is an expression of our love. How much do we have to give? How much do we really need? How much do we take with us?

♥ Love is committed. When we are committed, we are dedicated, faithful, and loyal.

♥ Love is renewing. Only love can make that which is sick, well, and old, new again.

♥ Love is work. Work is love. Love is about giving – giving is about work.

♥ Love is consoling. To console is to show compassion to another.

♥ Love is within. Love comes from within our hearts. *Seek, and ye shall find.*

♥ Love is healthy. The quality of love is good health. We are made to be healthy.

♥ Love is wisdom. Wisdom is love. As we grow in wisdom, we grow in love.

♥ Love is loving. Love produces love. As we love, we are loved.

♥ Love is our root program. We are programmed to love and to be loved.

♥ Love is a positive flow of energy. When we send love, we send positive energy.

♥ Love is content. As we evolve in consciousness, our priority changes from one of chasing our bliss, to that of finding contentment with what we have.

♥ Love is forever unfolding. Love is forever new.

We are here for the purpose of love. Life's most important lessons involve some aspect of love. We each determine the lesson plan for our lives based on our ability to love. To walk in love, we must know love. As wise, intelligent students seeking greater light, we ascend on the spiritual path by knowing love and walking in her truth

Affirmations of Love

Our reality is born of our thoughts. When our thoughts are filled with loving affirmations, we can manifest our love-filled dreams.

- ♥ I am a soul with a body.
- ♥ I am consciousness.
- ♥ I am a spirit being.
- ♥ I am a child of God.
- ♥ Reality is within me, then outside of me.
- ♥ I am here to serve.
- ♥ I am here to learn about and to grow in love.
- ♥ I am here to be an example to others.
- ♥ I am wonderfully made.
- ♥ I am here to enjoy all of nature.
- ♥ I am beautiful.
- ♥ I am filled with the light of God.
- ♥ I am here to share my light with others.
- ♥ I am here to grow.
- ♥ I am here to perfect my love.
- ♥ I am here to love and to be loved.
- ♥ I am a creative expression of my higher self.
- ♥ I have everything I need to express my light.
- ♥ I am able to overcome every challenge.
- ♥ I am perfectly healthy.
- ♥ My mind is sound, and my thoughts are clear.
- ♥ My heart is pure.
- ♥ I am ready to express my love and light

As we ascend in consciousness, we ascend in love. We ascend in consciousness by raising our thoughts into our higher chakras with thanks and gratitude. Practice the exercises below by closing your eyes and saying "thank you," to our creator for each high affirmation.

- ♥ Thank you for love. *I am love*
- ♥ Thank you for light. *I am light*
- ♥ Thank you for kindness. *I am kind*
- ♥ Thank you for freedom. *I am free*
- ♥ Thank you for goodness. *I am good*
- ♥ Thank you for patience. *I am patient*
- ♥ Thank you for peace. *I am peaceful*
- ♥ Thank you for wisdom. *I am wise*
- ♥ Thank you for compassion. *I am compassionate*
- ♥ Thank you for creativity. *I am creative*
- ♥ Thank you for happiness. *I am happy*
- ♥ Thank you for imagination. *I am imaginative*
- ♥ Thank you for joy. *I am joyful*
- ♥ Thank you for faith. *I am faithful*
- ♥ Thank you for Divine awareness. *I am aware*
- ♥ Thank you for enlightenment. *I am enlightened*
- ♥ Thank you for health. *I am healthful*
- ♥ Thank you for wholeness. *I am whole*
- ♥ Thank you for family. *I am family*
- ♥ Thank you for power. *I am powerful*
- ♥ Thank you for radiance. *I am radiant*
- ♥ Thank you for healing me. *I am healed*
- ♥ Thank you for nourishment. *I am nourished*

♥ Thank you for safety. *I am safe*

♥ Thank you for clarity. *I am clear*

♥ Thank you for change. *I am change*

♥ Thank you for devotion. *I am devoted*

♥ Thank you for nature. *I am nature*

♥ Thank you for music. *I am music*

The prayer of Ho'oponopono

The prayer of Ho'oponopono is a simple yet powerful prayer. Through forgiveness and love, we access the power of love. When praying for someone, for whatever reason, pray this short, yet powerful prayer.

I'm sorry. Please forgive me. Thank you. I love you.

HEART SCALE

With knowledge, wisdom, and understanding,
we change the weights and measures of our consciousness.

Love Weighs All Things – The heart scale gives us a means to weigh the matters of life. On one side of the scale, place the issue at hand: and on the other side, list the relevant virtues of love. We craft our lives with the decisions we make day by day. Knowledge and wisdom of a particular matter help us make good decisions for our lives. Once we are able to identify which chakra we are looking to satisfy and the motive for any particular action, we are able to make the best choice with proper consideration. If love is at the heart of our consideration, then we are probably on the right track.

Our perspective changes things – If we view the matters of life as lessons to be learned or to be taught, then the matter becomes just another one of many lessons we will eventually get. As Divinely-inspired students of love, seeking balance within our lives, we are subject to making wrong decisions. Often, our greatest lessons are learned through making wrong decisions. Making wrong decisions and failing in life is part of the process. We all learn a little differently.

We are here to peel the onion – As an onion has many layers, we have layer after layer of lessons to learn in life. Once we learn one lesson, there is another one just around the corner. We are here to learn the many lessons about life and love. Every day we learn something new and grow a little wiser. Some lessons are harder than others. An easy lesson for you may be a great trial for me. As we learn each lesson, we can count on the fact that there will be another lesson on the way. Failing lessons in life is part of the learning process. Serving punishment or revenge to a student for failing a lesson is illogical, wrong, and does not help the student, or better community. Community is best served when each corrective lesson is relative to the offense.

We are all here trying to figure things out. Seeking the truth is what set me on the path to love. It's important that we know the reality of life. It's important that we follow our greater integrity. It's important that we make the best of the short time we have here in Earth school. It's important that we honor one another as the spiritual brothers and sister that we are. It's important that we do the best we can.

PART SEVEN
A New Dream for Humanity

"The day will come when, after harnessing space, the winds,
the tides, and gravitation, we shall harness for God the energies of love.
And on that day, for the second time in the history
of the world, we shall have discovered fire."

- Pierre Teilhard de Chardin

THE NATURE OF INTEGRITY

When we build a framework of understanding
on a foundation of truth, our house will stand with integrity.

The topic of integrity is fundamental to all of us. What is more important than living an honest and truthful life? To walk with integrity is a virtue of love. From within the core of our beings, we want to live an honest, truthful life with all those around us. When we step out of our integrity for some reason, we are given a lesson to bring us back into alignment with our authentic selves. Living a life of integrity is essential to our health, survival, and spiritual growth.

What is integrity?

Integrity: The ethical concept of integrity is that of basing one's actions on a consistent framework of ethical principles. Integrity is a concept of consistency of actions, values, methods, measures, principles, expectations, and outcomes. In ethics, integrity is regarded as the honesty and truthfulness or accuracy of one's actions.

Integrity can be regarded as the opposite of hypocrisy, in that it regards internal consistency as a virtue and suggests that parties holding apparently conflicting values should account for the discrepancy or alter their beliefs.

The word "integrity" stems from the Latin adjective, integer (whole, complete). In this context, integrity is the inner sense of "wholeness" deriving from qualities such as honesty and consistency of character."
– Wikipedia

The ChakraKey represents a framework of ethical and honest principles based on the reality of our human spiritual construction. By understanding our inner design as represented by our chakra system, we are able to maintain consistency of actions, values, methods, measures, expectations, and outcomes.

The only way we can honestly address and manage the many issues we face in life with integrity is to bring the matters of our lives into alignment with each one of our chakras. Without understanding the nature of our chakra system and our inner programming, the powerful forces within our lower drives will confound our better reasoning.

Awareness is the key to Integrity.

Integrity is Wholeness: Knowledge and wisdom of our human spiritual design will help us to maintain our whole system with integrity. Balance is the key to peace and harmony.

To maintain the integrity of our *whole self*, we must understand the energetic nature of each of our seven chakras. We are wonderfully made with a giant heart chakra to help us naturally find balance and maintain equilibrium. Yet still, we are subject to diversion from the many issues we face in life. Conflicts will always be with us. Our great challenge, our great joy, and our great gift as human beings is the ability to manage dual energies and use them in a creative way for the greater good.

Bad programming makes for dysfunctional lives. Problems arise when we are taught to do things that are in conflict with our higher nature, by people we trust, honor, and whose truth we accept as the truth, even when it is not the truth.

Man has long been manipulating man for selfish reasons. The man with the most knowledge has the greatest advantage. Knowledge is power. The more intelligent the slaves, the more difficult they are to control. Man's drive for power over other men has long been a problem for humanity. When will we discover that we are all in this together? We are all one. What we do for another, we do for ourselves. Together, we will build a better world.

How can we determine for certain that which is good and true, and that which is false, or a lie? The idea of defining what is honest, truthful, and accurate can lead us in a variety of directions, depending upon our compass. Finding the truth and the balance of the many issues we face in life can be a daunting task. It can be a matter of trickery as well.

The ChakraKey and ChakraSynergy symbols provide us with the truth of our human spiritual design. The path to awareness begins with acknowledging our Divine nature and then growing in the radiance of our Divine purpose. If we are to live a life of integrity, we must acknowledge who we are and why we are here and set our intention to be about the business of living out our life purpose. Conscious awareness of our inner programming gives us power to creatively use the body as a tool to accomplish our greater dreams.

Personal Alignment

"Know thyself."

– Socrates

ChakraKey is a compass with a known point of center, from which we are able to recognize degrees of deviation when we wander off the path for any reason. With an understanding of our inner design, we are able to find balance within a sometimes turbulent sea of options for our lives.

Walking in truth and integrity is fundamental to living a joy-filled life. We will not find contentment or happiness until we are in alignment with our true selves and the world around us. So what does it mean to be in alignment? How do I know when I am alignment with my higher purpose?

We can use the wisdom of ChakraSynergy to help us maintain alignment with every issue we face. For example, my water supply has been poisoned. Do I drink the water or not?

Pro: I need water to survive.

Con: The available water has been poisoned and may kill me.

Law: The law of love compels me to love my body by only drinking pure, clean water.

Outcome: Purify the water or look elsewhere for water that is safe to drink.

This basic example illustrates the importance of integrity, alignment, and knowing the laws of love so that we might survive in a healthy way. We are governed by the laws of love. We must learn these laws and abide by them with every ounce of our ability. We can make decisions based on sound wisdom, or we can take the time to learn a life lesson. Growing in knowledge and wisdom of truth is the preferable method of course. Time is of the essence for all of us. We have suffered long enough. We are ready for a party. The party begins when we take personal responsibility for our light; when together we come into alignment with love; when together we imagine a new dream for humanity. We live in a complex world, and we face complex issues. Many social issues are even more complex than the physical issues of science and construction. The ChakraKey gives us a hierarchy of reasoning we can apply to the issues we face in life. We now have a means to bring integrity of thought and reason to all things.

If we are to evolve in a loving way here on Earth, we will do so because we establish loving rules and principles that are fair and just for all. Our weights, scales, and measures must be accurate, honest, and true. The rules we live by must survive the light of day, or they must be abolished.

While we must love our bodies in a healthy way, we are not here to just serve the body. We are here to grow in wisdom and understanding of all things around us and to be an expression of our Divine nature. When we live our life with this understanding, this purpose, and following this action, we are living a life of integrity.

In the arena of ideas, parties holding conflicting values should account for their discrepancies or alter their beliefs. Ideas and plans we feed together as a community with our time, money, and love, should bear the test of love. The laws, rules, and actions we live by must bear the full light of day, or they should be abandoned for ideas that support higher aspirations of human endeavor, including survival, balance, love, education, the arts, music, expression, and communion with the Divine.

We should collectively say **no** to people who seek to control and manipulate others for their own personal profit. We are here for the purpose of love. We may cause no intentional harm to any person without causing the same harm to ourselves.

Our path to integrity begins with our personal enlightenment. We become enlightened when we are able to see past the physical body and into the oneness of the true self. We become aware of our oneness by going within, through meditation, prayer, and connecting with Divine consciousness.

THE LAW OF WORK

"Work is not a burden to bear, but a gift to share."

The Law of Work is the law of circulation.
The Law of circulation is the Golden Rule in action.

The Golden Rule describes a cycle of action.
As love is a flow of giving and receiving,
work is a flow of giving and receiving.

Work provides us with a means of sharing our gifts of "love" with one another.
When we work, we are giving.
When we are paid, we are receiving.

A healthy work relationship involves a fair trade of giving and receiving.
Ultimately our motive for work is not about profit. Our motive for work is to share and express that which is within each of us.
We are here on Earth to be an expression of our whole selves. Work gives us the opportunity to serve and to share our particular gifts with those we love.

The Law of Work is a cycle of action.
The energy of work should equal the energy of compensation.

As we work with and for one another, we create a synergy of greater energy.
Money provides us with a versatile means of sharing the *labors of our love* with others.

The objective of community should be to create, maintain, and promote a network of healthy, energetic, working relationships, whereby everyone has some job to do.

- **Work is required for healthy communities.**
- **To create healthy communities, we make all of our own consumable products.**
- **To produce the best, safest, healthiest products, our community colleges should teach about every product we use in the community.**
- **We learn to produce everything we need to survive and to thrive.**
- **As we learn together and work together, we grow together in love.**

As love is a flow of giving and receiving, work is a flow of giving and receiving. When we buy products or services from other cities, states, or countries, we stop the flow of love within the local community. In the hierarchy of things, our personal survival and harmony within our community are our first responsibility. As we grow in abundance from within, we may share without.

Work provides the community with the fertile soil by which love grows through the sharing of one another's time, talent, and creative expression. A healthy community is one where everyone has a job sharing some aspect of his or her ability with others. As there are many flowers in the fields, we are many souls, here to participate in life's adventure.

As gifted human spiritual beings, our great desire is to express our love, our skill, and our ability in some way. We do this best through our work.

- As artists, our joy is to create art.
- As builders, our joy is to build.
- As engineers, our joy is to engineer.
- As farmers, our joy is to farm.
- As teachers, our joy is to teach.
- As doctors, our joy is to heal.
- As musicians, our joy is to play music.
- As architects, our joy is to design.
- As dancers, our joy is to dance.
- As singers, our joy is to sing.
- Our joy is to be what we must be. This is our integrity.

Work is about sharing your gifts and talents with someone in a purposeful way.

Work is our sacred calling.
The path is about service.

Mentor Method of Education

A Love-Based Method of Education

The mentor method of education is a "love-based" instructional program based upon the natural laws of love. As love is a flow of giving and receiving, the teacher-student relationship is a flow of giving and receiving.

Features of the "mentor method" of education:

- As a teacher, one has the opportunity to share knowledge, wisdom, and experience with the student. This giving is love.

- As a student, one has the opportunity to receive knowledge, wisdom, and experience from a teacher. This receiving is also love.

- As the student becomes the teacher and shares knowledge with another student, this giving is love.

- The student teacher, teacher-student relationship naturally creates a flow of love.

- To grow in love is the preferred result of all transactions and relationships.

To teach a subject, one must know the subject. As a teacher, one has a responsibility to understand the subject of any given lesson. As a student prepares to put on the hat of a teacher, he or she is inspired to understand the material in great detail, to help the fellow student. We are motivated to learn that we might be able to give. As we thirst to receive, we thirst to give.

My teacher, my role model – As teachers, we are role models. Younger students are inspired to learn from their peers. Inspiration and perspective change everything.

As spiritual beings, we resonate with, and we are drawn to people with similar interests, gifts, and abilities. Birds of a feather flock together for a reason.

There are many kinds of flowers in the garden.

- Artists learn best from other artists.
- Engineers learn best from other engineers.
- Mathematicians learn best from other mathematicians.
- Writers learn best from other writers.
- Musicians learn best from other musicians.
- Dancers learn best from other dancers.

Chemistry and compatibility: For mentors and the mentored, chemistry, compatibility, and passion are essential to building strong relationships. Like-minded people resonate with one another. When energies match, there is energy connection that feels right. When energies are off, we feel uncomfortable and would prefer to leave. People learn best from others like them, within a fun and inspiring work environment.

As good students, we know "where our attention goes, our energy flows." As we manage our attention, we manage our energy. Areas of our lives we choose to feed are the areas of our lives that we choose to grow. As we consciously and continually grow the higher aspirations of our lives, our efforts manifest into our greater dreams.

When love is the engine that drives our motivation, we become a powerful force of inspiration.

We are at our best when we are inspired by a subject, a project, a creation, or manifesting a dream. As teachers, it is our job to help students discover/identify their natural gifts and then use these gifts in an inspiring way.

Inspiration is the key to education. We all want to do what we enjoy doing. We enjoy doing what we do well. Granted, sometimes we desire to do something we find difficult, in order to master a particular art. This is also good.

As love is free, children and adults should be free to choose the vocation of their passion. We should not be forced to learn topics that do not resonate with our current aspirations.

We are here to learn and master the many lessons of life.

PICK ME UP WHEN I FALL

Falling, failing, and flailing are all part of learning. When I fail at something, help me to see the error and make the correction. Thank you for loving me when I am not so loveable. I realize I have much to learn. Please be patient with me if I stumble. I am made with great ability to learn and to love. Love is at the core of my being. If I make a series of very bad decisions, or if I become involved with a substance that overtakes my ability for rational reason, please help me to help myself. Do not give up on me. Do not lock me away in chains and forget about me. Help me, educate me, and teach me the ways of love. The love, compassion, and kindness you show me will return to you some day, in some beautiful way.

"One man's ceiling is another man's floor."

-Paul Simon

A NEW DREAM FOR HUMANITY

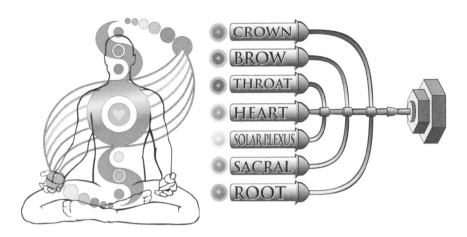

"Humanity is going to require a substantially new way of thinking if it is going to survive."

Albert Einstein

Within our world, we face complex issues that affect millions of lives. The time has come to observe nature's way, and restructure our world around organizing principles, based on Mother Nature's natural harmonies. ChakraKey opens the door to new thought, new ideas, and a new framework of design that we can use to build a new culture *Harmoniously Integrated* with Mother Nature. As Mother Nature is made of layer upon layer of *Harmoniously Integrated Systems*, we now have a framework we can use to redesign social structures to interlink with one another and with Mother Nature.

Sorting out the many complex issues we face on Earth without a means of organization is futile. Taking a cue from Mother Nature, we now have a way to organize the many issues of life in an objective, organized, balanced way.

Living the dream of our consciousness - As there is a full spectrum of color within the rainbow and chakra system, there is a full spectrum of human spiritual beings here on Earth, each wanting to express life in their own colorful way. Musical notes of like tones resonate together, just as like-minded and like-energy people resonate together. This is natural. Given there are people in our world of every level of consciousness, together we must create educational programs designed to elevate the tone and consciousness of those living in the lower centers. Our common objective is ascension for all beings.

Each human being has hopes and dreams related to their level of consciousness. A dream for one may be a nightmare for another. Dreams come in many forms, depending on one's environment, creative ability, and level of consciousness:

- Some dream of having enough food, water, and shelter to survive.
- Some dream of having sex all of the time.
- Some dream of having more money or power.
- Some dream to serve others in love.
- Some dream of learning and to be heard.
- Some dream of being able to express creative artistic endeavors
- Some dream of joining in oneness with God.

Not all dreams are good for us. Dreams, hopes, and aspirations must be weighed for the beneficial value for the whole. Dreams by those living within the lower centers of consciousness must be carefully weighed. *If our common objective is love, then we manage dreams from the lower centers, while encouraging dreams to flourish from the high centers.*

For instance: The dream for one to rule all of the lands and have an abundance of slaves and concubines for one's personal pleasure is a fairly common dream for men. Of course, this dream might be a nightmare for others. As a community, we must be careful of the dreams that we allow to grow in our world. As dreams crystallize into reality, they take on energy that is often difficult to stop without great pain and suffering. Slavery, for instance, is an old dream that took years of struggling and fighting to stop in America. Slavery remains alive and well today in many countries. Children are often raised with ideas they sense to be wrong, yet are firmly held by their parents, family, and friends as true and good. These confusing values and behaviors appear as normal, and they grow into the energy of wrongness.

Social structures we allow to exist that are not of love become a cancer to the body. As a community, we must recognize the many forms of cancer growing within us and stop them, fill them with love, change them, rearrange them, or cut them out if necessary. There is no benefit for the body to willingly allow harmful elements to grow within itself. This would not be love; this would not be kind. This would not be the responsible thing to do.

There is a great competition for what dreams may come. In the arena of ideas, there is a great competition for power and control over the many assets of the earth. Those in control seek to remain in control, regardless of the outcome or harm they do to anyone, and those who have no power of control seek the power and control from others. There is a never-ending competition for control and power underway. This competition has led us from brutal war to brutal war.

The reality is, we are all here for a short time. Like a flower, we are born, we grow and bud into our beautiful radiance, and then we wilt and die. During our time we are in a constant state of evolving and growing. It is for this reason, we should create social structures designed to serve humankind that will live on for generation after generation. The idea here is to create social structures designed to facilitate the loving evolution of humankind without the need for senseless war after war. We cannot kill or harm another soul without a very good reason of self-defence. When we do so, part of us dies with that person. Wars are very mean games by selfish people. The time has come for humanity to put down the weapons, and look to one another as brothers and sisters of one love. There is enough to go around. War is not the answer for an enlightened civilization. Love is the only sustainable path.

We know that what we feed is what grows, physically and energetically. If love, peace, and happiness is the objective for all life, then let's build social systems designed to facilitate this experience. As a loving, energized social network, we can bring our energy together to form super-electromagnet energy of transformation to our social surroundings. Imagine the world we might create with Love, Peace, and Harmony as our common objective?

Our vision of the world and what we might become is limited to what we think is possible. As we grow in knowledge, wisdom, and understanding of love and our Divine nature, we are empowered with a new understanding of things. As a great society of most intelligent, spiritual beings, with a direct connection to Divine consciousness, there is nothing that we cannot do, change, or create. We only have to understand the game, to change the game. Up until now, the game has been a mystery.

The rules to the game of life need not be a mystery. While we have much to learn, may we grow from understanding the basic realities of life. *When we build a framework of understanding on a foundation of truth, our house will stand with integrity.* Now that I know the truth, I will play the game differently.

The game of life should no longer be a mystery. We now have a guide to keep us pointed in the right direction. While there is still much to learn, we now have the basics rules for the game of life.

- Now I know it's all about love.
- Now I know it's all about energy, and how I use and manage my energy.
- Now I know how to prioritize my attention.
- Now I know the rules of the game of life.
- Now I know what I need to do with my life.
- Now I know why I am here, and my purpose in life.

- Now I know how to distinguish between the desires of my body and the higher aspirations of my spirit nature.
- Now I know what to dream about.
- Now I know what integrity means.
- Now I know where to find God.
- Now I know the importance of education.
- Now I know the importance of teaching others about love.
- Now I know the importance of giving.
- Now I know the value of knowledge and wisdom.
- Now I know the importance of not taking more than I need.
- Now I know the importance of honoring the Earth, and Mother Nature.
- Now I know the importance of spending time in prayer and meditation.
- Now I know the importance of being true to myself.
- Now I know the importance of loving my family.
- Now I know the importance of sharing what I have learned about love with others.
- Now I know the importance of honoring sexual relationships.
- Now I know the value of money.
- Now I know the importance of singing, playing music and joyful dance.
- Now I know the joy of fellowship and unconditional love.
- Now I know the joy of co-creating new dreams with friends.

As one who knows, it is my responsibility, honor, and duty to help others live a more loving life. As compassionate human beings, may we dedicate our lives to the purpose of building a new love-based society. We are intelligent, industrious, gentle, loving people, here to raise families and live our lives in peace and harmony. We now have an incredible new model of design we can apply to every aspect of our lives. Now is the time to dream a new dream for the quicker evolution of humanity.

- Now is the time for love
- Now is the time for peace
- Now is the time to create a unified Earth School
- Now is the time for teachers of love, to teach about love.
- Now is the time to collectively join hearts embracing our oneness.
- Now is the time to honor one another as spiritual beings of Divine creation.
- Now is the time to bring love to the mass media.
- Now is the time to live with a greater integrity.
- Now is the time to rebuild our social systems.
- Now is the time to rethink commerce.
- Now is the time to rethink government.

We face complex issues in our world today. Life and death are at hand within every moment of every day. With our new understanding of energy, life, and love, we can become a force of love, through changing the energy associated with ever issue we face. We shed light on lower energy ideas until the energy is changed into love. Love affects change in a loving way. We grow in love as we grow in wisdom, knowledge, and understanding of love. Education about love is fundamental for our children, young teens, and people of all ages.

We do better when we know better.

As you grow in love, you will have a better sense of what is good and loving and what is not. Soon you will learn which thoughts and actions to feed in your life, and which not to feed. The lower yang forces of old tradition and thought are powerful and may take some time to bring into alignment with your spirit nature so be patient with yourself. Now that you know, you will grow.

I hope this information will inspire you to look at love in a new light. We all have a role to play in the evolution of love throughout humanity. The role you play in the unfolding of love is up to you. May your life be filled with love and light.

If this book has helped you, please share it with others. The greatest gift you can share with someone is to help them find themselves. As one grows in light, we all grow into a greater light. As we collectively grow in light, awareness, and love, we will create a critical mass of light that will transform the world.

One voice is easily lost in the chaos of life. A million voices cannot be ignored. While darkness may extinguish a single candle, a forest fire, burning with a multitude of passionate hearts, brings light to the darkness. Join me, my friend, lift your torch of love, and let us ignite a forest fire of enlightenment that will forever shine in the hearts of humankind.

We come as light bearers! We are all children of the light. We are all blessed with Divine light and goodness within each of our hearts. May your light grow, as you help others to grow their light. Light produces light.

Love is forever changing,
Love is forever new,
Love is forever me,
Love is forever you.

In service to love,
Rick Ireton

Appendix

Personal Assessment
Finding Your Light

"Inspiration without action is merely entertainment."

Mary Morrissey

The first step to finding your life path begins with self-evaluation. We begin by taking inventory of our physical, mental, and spiritual assets. We can do this by asking a few basic questions. Answer from the core of your being; from your truth.

1. If time and money were not an issue, what would you love to do?

2. Considering what you love to do, what is the most loving thing you have to share with the world?

3. Knowing that you are here to be an expression of love, and you are gifted with many talents, what can you do right now to be most helpful?

Important rules to remember:

- Where your attention goes, your energy flows.
- What you feed, is what grows.
- The energy you send around comes around.
- The law of forgiveness. – As we forgive others, we release them, and we are forgiven.
- Our great power is found within our hearts, our voices, our minds, and our connection with divine consciousness. We exercise this power by sending our ideas, thoughts, and desires to others through our connection with Divine consciousness, with hearts filled with thanks and gratitude for the desired outcome.
- As physical exercise produces physical rewards, spiritual exercise produces spiritual rewards.

So who are you? What do you love to do? What would you love to share with others? How can you help? What can you best give to others?

Thinking back to your childhood, what events brought you the most pleasure?

- Do you love mechanical things?
- Do you love to read?
- Do you enjoy mathematics?
- Do you possess a gift of music?
- Do you have a great desire to communicate?
- Do you love the arts, to paint, to sculpt, and to make things with your hands?
- Do you like to build things?
- Do you like to work with your hands in the soil and to grow things?

- Do you like medicine and the idea of helping people?
- Do you like to teach and share your wisdom of love with others?

As young students, we should give our attention to the things in life that inspire us. If you are drawn to art, spend your time drawing and developing your artistic skills. We know we are on the path of truth and love when we follow the inspirations from within our hearts. Because we are so multi-talented, we tend to grow in one area for a while and then in another. This is all part of the lesson plan for our lives.

Some ideas to help your dreams come true:

- Follow your own dreams.
- Write down your dream today.
- Commit to your dream.
- Think it, speak it, and desire it every day.
- Transcend the dream and become the dream.
- Feed the dream with your attention. Where your attention goes, your energy flows.
- Surround yourself with others who share your dreams and inspirations.
- Tomorrow begins today. Hold your intentions and prayers within your dreams.
- Your history does not control your destiny. Each day you are given the chance to chart a new course for your life.

Steps to manifesting your dreams:

1. What is your dream? (Be specific.)
2. Does it involve love?
3. Does your dream align with your core values?
4. Does it require you to expand your knowledge base?

5. Will you need help from a higher power?

6. Do you want to receive what you are giving away?

7. What is your greater intention?

8. What obstacles are in your way?

9. How will you overcome them?

We are all in transition. Your thoughts about life today will be different tomorrow. As you grow in knowledge and wisdom, you will transform your life into an ever-growing vision of yourself. With each day of life, we plant new seeds of thoughts and actions. Each thought and every action grows into something that serves us, becomes work, or becomes a new lesson to learn. We are all as farmers, and we will surely reap what we sow. May you reap a plentiful harvest of a life well lived, and well loved.

ChakraSynergy Work Sheet

Let Love be Your Guide

Topic _____

Crown
Is this a good dream?
Will this decision lead to greater unity?
Can we live in peace with this decision?

Brow
Do I know all of the facts?
What is the wise thing to do?
Is this a good creative choice?

Throat
What is the logical thing to do?
Can I speak to this decision in the light of day?
Will this improve my creative expression?

Heart
How does my heart feel about this?
What is the lesson?
Will this decision stand the test of love?
What is the loving thing to do?
Will this decision bring me love?

Solar plexus
Will this decision empower me?
What is my motive for this decision?
How will this affect my safety and security?

Sacral
What does my gut say?
Will this bring me pleasure?
Will this bring balance to my life?

Root
Can I live with this decision?
How will this decision affect my survival?
Will this connect me to Mother Earth?

From time to time we face difficult issues in our life.
Use the Chakra Synergy Worksheet to help you make the most important
decisions of your life. Our decisions matter.

Use the ChakraSynergy work sheet to make the most important decisions of your life. The human spiritual being is uniquely made with the ability to manage and bring balance to opposing forces, by virtue of our energetic design. Now that we understand this framework of design, we can apply this technology to our life and our communities. We can see the framework of our most intelligent design in the ChakraSynergy symbol. Generic questions relating to each chakra center have been added to the left side of the symbol design form. These questions are subject to change of course as they may relate to you.

Note: Before getting started, make a copy of the questionnaire so you can use a copy whenever you are faced with an important question you need to resolve in a loving way. If you need another copy of the worksheet, go to www.chakrakey.com for a free copy.

The purpose of the work sheet is to bring the issues we face in life into the full spectrum of color inquiry. Now that we know what love looks and feels like, we can choose love, knowing that we have done our best.

ChakraSynergy Work Sheet Instructions:

1. Write down your question/topic at the top of the page.

2. Beginning at the root chakra, bring your topic to each question relating to your survival. For instance: If your question is, should I join the military?

   Question A. Can I live with this decision?

   Question B. How will this decision affect my survival?

   Question C. Will this connect me to Mother Earth?

3. As you fill out the questionnaire, some questions will carry a greater weight of importance for you. Take time to reflect upon the significance of each question noting the limitation of the chakra. The heart chakra will, of course, be given the greatest measure of weight.

The work sheet will help you to perceive the possible outcome of your action or lack of action should you carry out the intended plan. If we are to move in the direction of love, we must be able to perceive what that move looks like and how that will impact our lives. We two basic options:

Love weighs all things. We will make the best decisions for our life when we take the time to account for the whole matter, not just one or two aspects of the matter. The more we understand an issue, the better we will be able to make productive, creative, love-based decisions. Love does not have to be an intangible emotional desire. There is logic to love that we can apply to our life in a very practical way.

We change our life, by changing the way we make decisions.

If we are to create more love in our life and in the world, we will do so by making more love-based decisions. *The process / program by which we make decisions in our life, and allow others to make decisions for us is vitally important. Within the formula or program, lies the outcome of our life and for the evolution of humanity.*

If our root program is based on the high-ways of love, knowledge, wisdom, and truth, humanity will organically grow and evolve in a loving way here on Earth.

If our root program is based upon the lower pursuit of survival, sex, and power, humanity will continue to suffer through needless war after war as we have for thousands of years.

Love, harmony, balance, peace, compassion, creativity is the root program of the human spiritual being. May we adopt this program of design for our life and our communities.

A love-based program is the key, to the loving evolution of humanity.

When love is our program, our program will be love.

CHAKRA IMAGING SYSTEMS

Until recent years, our knowledge of chakras came from Hindu masters, who through meditation were able to see their chakra centers as colorful vortices of color-energy. Writings on chakras go back to the Vedas, produced over 4,000 years ago.

Today there are a variety of imaging systems able to measure and display a person's aura and chakra centers based upon biofeedback information and Kirlian photography. (Kirlian photography is a photographic technique used to capture the phenomenon of electrical coronal discharges.)

Aura Video Station - The Aura Video Station is an Interactive Multimedia Biofeedback System based on the principles of Biofeedback, Color Psychology, Energy, and Mind/Body Medicine. The Aura Video Station uses biofeedback sensors to measure, analyze, and process the biofeedback data of the energetic and activity levels of the client. This bio data is correlated with specific emotional-energetic states and then displayed on the screen.

How does it work? The client's hand is laid on the Bio Sensor, which analyzes and correlates the information and feeds it to the computer. The data is then displayed on the screen as a representation of the client's aura in full pulsating color. Biofeedback also uses the measured data as graphs and charts that illustrate reactions and changes taking place in the aura and chakras.

What the Client Sees: Clients can watch their auras in motion! The Aura Video Station shows not only the personality patterns but also the client's thought fields and the actual changes that are happening in his or her day-to-day life. You might see aura changes during therapy or healing session, while talking to another person, after using different healing products or tools, during meditation or visualization, etc. Basically, the aura will change whenever an emotional, mental, or energetic change is created within or around a person! For more information on the Aura Video Station visit: **www.aura.net**

Psy-Tek Labs – provides companies, individuals, or health practitioners who make new health devices or products, or offer services that are not based on the allopathic model of health care (and so need validation,) with the expertise to validate the effectiveness of their new health devices, or products or services, through rigorously designed research studies.

Why do research? Research projects involving human subjects are under strict regulations by the Food and Drug Administration (FDA). The FDA assigns the task of reviewing and approving research projects to Institutional Review Boards (IRBs), which are formed by experts in fields related to the health sciences and are required to follow strictly, FDA guidance. For more information about the various methods of energetic testing available visit www.psy-tek.com

ABOUT THE AUTHOR

Rick has a passion for love. Since discovering the significance of love in 2002, Rick has dedicated his life to researching love in all of its many forms. Finding the ChakraKey and ChakraSynergy symbols have opened a door of new exploration about love. Love is a complicated matter, having many definitions. The ChakraKey gives us a new framework to better understand love in all its many forms.

Rick is motivated by love, to share what he has discovered with all who will listen. Love has been off the radar of our consciousness for too long. Now is the time for love.

If you are as inspired by love as Rick, take action by participating in one of the love-based organizations below.

www.lovepeaceandfreedom.org - Love, Peace & Freedom Foundation is dedicated to producing educational materials about our human spiritual design and love. The more we know about love, the more we will love one another.

www.chakrakey.com – for books, DVDs, and ChakraSynergy T-Shirts

www.loveparty.org – The Love Party is dedicated to promoting a Love-based philosophy for life, based upon wisdom found within the ChakraKey.

BIBLIOGRAPHY

Alex Jones, *Seven Mansions of Color*, Marina Del Ray: DeVorss & Company, 1982

Carolyn Myss, *Anatomy of the Spirit*, New York, NY: Harmony Books, 1996

Charles Johnston, *The Yoga Sutras of Patanjali*, Stuart and Watkins, London, England, 1968

Don Miguel Ruiz, *The Mastery of Love*, Amber-Allen Publishing, 1999

Eric Butterworth, *Life is for Love*, Harper & Row, New York, NY, 1973

Ernest Holmes, *Love & Law*, The Unpublished Teachings, New York, NY, Penguin Group, 2004

Gary Zukav, *Seat of the Soul*, 1230 Avenue of the Americas, New York, NY 10020, Fireside, 1990

James Oschman, *Energy Medicine*, Churchill Livingstone, Edinburgh London, 2000

Jerry Tennant, *Healing is Voltage, The Handbook*, 2010

Liz Simpson, *Chakra Healing*, New York, NY, Sterling Publishing Company, 1999

Rudolf Steiner, *Spiritual Hierarchies*, Anthroposophic Press, Hudson, NY, 1996

Savitri Simpson, *Chakras for Starters*, Crystal Clarity Publishers, Nevada City, CA, 2010

Susan Wright, *The Chakras in Shamanic Practice*, Destiny Books, Rochester, VT, 2007

Taylor G Bunch, *Love*, Review and Harold, Washington DC, Copyright 1952

Thich Nhat Hanh, *Teachings on Love*, Parallax Press, Berkley, CA, 2007

Yogananda Paramahansa, *The Autobiography of a Yogi*, Los Angeles, CA Self-Realization Fellowship, 1971